HUNTING THE WIND

PAN AMERICAN WORLD AIRWAYS' EPIC FLYING BOAT ERA, 1929–1946

Schiffer Publishing Ltd

4880 Lower Valley Road • Atglen, PA 19310

Other Schiffer Books on Related Subjects:

Boeing 737: The World's Jetliner, by Captain Dan Dornseif, 978-0-7643-5325-3

Air 200: Aircraft of the US Bicentennial, by Wayne Mutza, 978-0-7643-0388-3

Restoring Museum Aircraft, by Robert Mikesh, 978-0-7643-3234-0

Designed by Justin Watkinson

The front cover by renowned aviation artist, Ron Cole,
depicts a Pan Am S-42 flying over the Golden Gate Bridge in 1935.

Type set in Bodoni MT/Minion Pro/Univers LT Std

ISBN: 978-0-7643-5541-7
Printed in China

Published by Schiffer Publishing, Ltd.
4880 Lower Valley Road
Atglen, PA 19310
Phone: (610) 593-1777; Fax: (610) 593-2002
E-mail: Info@schifferbooks.com
Web: www.schifferbooks.com

For our complete selection of fine books on this and related subjects, please visit our
website at www.schifferbooks.com. You may also write for a free catalog.

Schiffer Publishing's titles are available at special discounts for bulk purchases for
sales promotions or premiums. Special editions, including personalized covers,
corporate imprints, and excerpts, can be created in large quantities for special needs.
For more information, contact the publisher.

We are always looking for people to write books on new and related subjects.
If you have an idea for a book, please contact us at proposals@schifferbooks.com.

CONTENTS

Foreword

by Julia Cooke

Beneath the iconic blue globe logo, amid the bustle of the 1980s Pan Am Terminal at JFK, my mother, father, sister, and I used to stand in front of the departures board and decide where to go on vacation. The bags on the floor alongside us were packed with hot or cold "standby supplies," and any plane with four open seats was fair game. My parents would be due back at work on Monday or maybe Tuesday if it was a long weekend.

Much of my childhood lore revolves around one fact: My father worked for Pan Am until I was nine. That's how old I was when the company folded in 1991.

Pan Am's demise was a crumpling-in that scattered employees, passengers, and infrastructure across other airlines and industries. In the popular imagination, it signified not just bankruptcy, but the end of an age. Air travel shifted, and the "blue globe device," as my father called it, came to symbolize a moment in time.

The Pan Am logo also symbolized a community. For members of that community, for the writers of this book (remarkably including three former flying boat crewmembers) and for my family, the change that occurred when Pan Am went under was both global and personal. Like thousands of other Pan Am employees and their families, our travels would never again be as spontaneous, glamorous, or exciting. Certainly it would not sparkle with serendipitous adventures. (Ask my mother about the time we went to the Caribbean and the only available hotel was a nudist colony!)

As a writer, I grew interested in Pan Am in 2014, when I started attending functions of the Pan Am Historical Foundation. My interest began as quizzical and intellectual. How had the employees of Pan Am practiced globalization before it was even really a term? If Pan Am was indeed a large, extended clan, I was meeting long-lost aunties and uncles who had entertained and ministered to me on transoceanic flights, who'd held my hand while guiding me to visit the cockpit, and who inspired a career couched largely in travel.

As I've gotten to know more and more former employees and their descendants, affectionately called "Pan Am babies," I've seen that Pan Am provided formative experiences, security, discovery, cherished relationships, and the ability to become oneself—a family.

In truth, I don't remember standing in front of the JFK departures board. Much as I like that image, I can't claim it. Between the repetition of family anecdotes and details I know to be true from childhood, my mind has tricked me. Yet the memories of new destinations and the travel itself—broad Pan Am seats, murmuring passengers, and glimmering city lights far below—remain very much alive.

The gulf between childhood and adult comprehension is broad, and understanding Pan Am's history is a task with consequences both intellectual and intimate. Take this book, for example. I knew almost nothing about Pan Am's brief but legendary flying boats, the essential roles they played in the development of modern aviation, how vital they were to the outcome of WWII, their plush onboard services and exquisite terminals, and the pioneering men and women who created and operated them.

Clearly, I have much to learn. So I'll keep going to Pan Am events, listening to tales of routines and adventures, and through books like *Hunting the Wind*, I'll soak in what I can of the history of an airline and its people—the Pan Am phenomenon that will likely never be repeated.

The Meaning of "Hunting the Wind"

Ken Follett's gripping spy novel *Night Over Water* (1991) takes place on board a Pan Am Boeing B-314 while crossing the north Atlantic. In it, he explains: "The crucial factor was the strength of the wind. The westward trip was a constant battle against the prevailing wind. Pilots would change altitude constantly in a search for the most favorable conditions, a game known as 'hunting the wind.' The lightest winds were generally found at lower altitudes, but below a certain point the plane would be in danger of colliding with ships or, more likely, icebergs. Strong winds required more fuel, and sometimes the forecast winds were so strong that the Clipper simply couldn't carry enough fuel to last the two thousand miles to Newfoundland."

From *West With the Night* by Beryl Markham (1942): "The wing does not want so much to fly true as to tug at the hands that guide it; the ship would rather hunt the wind than lay her nose to the horizon far ahead."

A further explanation from Pan Am captain Robert Gandt: "Hunting the wind was an essential form of fuel management for ocean-crossing flying boats. Because westward winds prevail in most of the world's oceans, it was the crew's urgent task to seek the least headwind when flying westbound and the maximum tailwind flying to the east. Finding the ideal wind at higher altitude or wave-top height often determined whether a flying boat had sufficient range to cross the ocean."

Acknowledgments

Without the ongoing patience and support from Doug Miller, webmaster of the Pan Am Historical Foundation (panam. org), use of the majority of photos depicted in this book would not have been possible.

The editors are also indebted to Barry O'Kelly, operations & records manager of the Foynes Flying Boat Museum, and to the museum's director and book contributor, Margaret O'Shaughnessy, for the use of the museum's archival images.

Former Pan Am captain Don Cooper graciously lent his knowledge and personal experience to various subjects, and Edward Trippe, son of Pan Am founder Juan Trippe and president of the Pan Am Historical Foundation, shared information not otherwise available.

In addition to two fascinating chapters in this book, author and former Pan Am captain Robert Gandt, helped to hold the project together at critical points. His advice and contributions were invaluable.

For their warm hospitality and assistance in accessing materials from the Pan Am Archives, our thanks to Cristina Favretto, head of Special Collections at the Richter Library, University of Miami; to Jay Sylvestre, Special Collections librarian; and to Yvette Yurubi, library assistant.

Carey Massimini, senior coordinator and assistant to Pete Schiffer, and senior editor Cheryl Weber were enormously helpful guiding us through the publishing process. Without their encouraging and immediate responses, this book would never have made it to print.

Deepest gratitude to all the contributors of this anthology who donated their knowledge, time, patience, and talents!

Finally, sincere thanks to our readers. We hope *Hunting the Wind* will entertain, educate, and transport you into Pan American's unparalleled flying boat era.

—TERESA WEBBER
chief editor/contributor coordinator

Contributors

TERESA TERRELL WEBBER (coordinator and chief editor) is the nonfiction author of internationally published travel and human interest articles, and *A Touch of First Class: Pan Am Recipes & Nostalgia* (2013). She flew as a stewardess for Pan Am for sixteen years, based in Miami, Los Angeles, and Honolulu. In college, Teresa studied Spanish and Hispanic culture in Oregon, Peru, and Spain. Previously, she lived with her family in Hawaii, Guam, and American Samoa. After twenty expat years in Bangkok and Manila, she now resides "back home" in Kaneohe, Hawaii, with her indulging husband and four rescue cats.

RON COLE (aviation artist) is a professional designer and businessman living with his wife and son in Zanesville, Ohio. He has photo-etched industrial products and worked in the film industry as a model maker, character designer, and artist. Ron also designed and constructed working models and prototypes for the toy industry. Working in the aerospace industry, Ron built both scale and full-size working models for the Jet Propulsion Laboratory (JPL), McDonnell Douglas, and other large companies. Among a long list of other accomplishments, Ron's art graced the pages of Pan Am's 2016 calendar. His business, Cole's Aircraft, has grown into the world's largest single-artist aviation/historical art web store with more than 35,000 followers on Facebook.

JAMIE DODSON (contributor, format and image editor) is the award-winning author of the historical fiction series The Nick Grant Adventures. In the four books—*Flying Boats & Spies*, *China Clipper*, *Mission: Shanghai*, and *Black Dragons Attack*—Jamie weaves fact with fiction, capturing the golden age of Pan Am's flying boats. He is also a career intelligence officer for the US Army and has taught aviation history at the University of Alabama in Huntsville. He writes nonfiction for aviation and military magazines, and speaks at writers' conferences, air shows, aviation museums, libraries, and schools across the nation.

ANN MARIE MARTIN (line editor) is a freelance writer and editor with more than thirty years' experience. An award-winning journalist, she was a feature writer and editor for the *Huntsville Times* in Huntsville, Alabama, for almost twenty-five years. During her last five years at the *Huntsville Times*, she wrote a biweekly column on books and writers, edited the weekly book page, and was head copyeditor on the news desk. She lives in Huntsville with her computer-programmer husband, Darren Fuemmeler, who helps manage her website, annmariemartin.ink, and their eight cats.

JULIA COOKE (contributor) writes from cities near and far (New York, Havana, Lisbon, Yangon, Mexico City) for *Conde Nast Traveler*, the *Virginia Quarterly Review*, *Saveur*, and many other magazines. She is the author of *The Other Side of Paradise: Life in the New Cuba* (Seal Press 2014) and the recipient of awards and honors from the New York Press Club and the Best American Travel Writing series. Photo credit Patrick Proctor

JEFF KRIENDLER (contributor) joined Pan Am in 1968, after graduation from Cornell University, where he later lectured. Following a broad avenue of experience spanning in-flight services and public relations, he was named vice president of corporate communications in 1982, remaining in that post until Pan Am's demise in 1991. Currently residing in Miami Beach, he is contributing editor for *Airways Magazine* and has produced three airline employee anthologies on Pan Am, Eastern Air Lines, and Trans World Airlines. Jeff's most recent book is *Pan Am: Personal Tributes to a Global Aviation Pioneer* (2017). His fifty-year career in aviation has provided painful lessons in crisis communications.

ROBERT GANDT (contributor) is a former naval officer, Pan Am captain, and award-winning novelist and historian. He is the author of sixteen books, including *Skygods: The Fall of Pan Am*, and the contemporary bestseller *The President's Pilot*. His screen credits include the television series *Pensacola: Wings of Gold*. Gandt's account of the WWII battle for Okinawa, *The Twilight Warriors*, was the winner of the prestigious Samuel Eliot Morison Award for Naval Literature. His 2017 nonfiction book is titled *Angels in the Sky*.

THOMAS KEWIN (contributor) came to Pan American as a flight engineer in March 1943, a twenty-year-old fresh out of the Boeing School of Aeronautics. He flew through WWII out of San Francisco and Honolulu and worked the last B-314 to San Francisco in April 1946. Tom stayed with Pan Am for forty years, accruing 31,000 hours of flight time. His 2005 book, *The Pan Am Journey*, is an accurate and entertaining look at the airline and its people. From the Sikorsky flying boats to the 747, Tom was there for it all.

ED DOVER (contributor) joined Pan American in November 1942 as a flight radio officer. Ed's fascinating book, *The Long Way Home*, is a perfect example of fact proving far more exciting than fiction. Following initial ground assignments at Pearl City and Noumea, New Caledonia, he remained on flight duty status, based in San Francisco until July 1945, when he transferred to the Africa-Orient Division of the flying Army Air Forces operations, based in New York. In January 1946, he took an assignment to Vienna, Austria, to help set up ground communications in preparation for Pan Am's post-war development of civilian airline services. After a year in Vienna, he returned to flight duty in New York. In the spring of 1948, when the position of flight radio operator was being phased out, Ed resigned from Pan Am. He signed on with the Civil Aeronautics Authority (now the Federal Aviation Administration) and worked as a flight service specialist and air traffic controller in Hawaii, Wake, Midway, Kansas City, St. Louis, and New Mexico until he retired from the FAA in 1982.

MERRY ATHEARN BARTON (contributor) is the daughter of Pan Am's former Noumea, New Caledonia, station manager. In December 1941, five-year-old Merry and her family were evacuated from Noumea by Pacific Clipper only days after the attack on Pearl Harbor. She is the only living passenger from that secretive round-the-world flight. Pieced together from early memories, as well as family photos and recordings made by her father, Merry's story captivates audiences at worldwide Pan Am reunions. Merry resides with husband John in Kamuela on the Big Island of Hawaii for half the year, and in San Rafael, California, for the other half of the year.

ROBERT HICKS (contributor) joined the Pacific Division of Pan Am at Treasure Island in August 1942 as a third officer, later as a first officer to fly the Boeing 314 Clippers. After transferring to the Latin America Division in Miami, he completed pre-command training, but with no captain openings, he flew one year as copilot on the DC-3. Because of his Pan Am experience and his BS and MBA degrees from Stanford, Walt Disney later hired him as a project manager. His first assignment was to establish a corporate aircraft operation, and to recommend the first airplane and pilot for the company. Now in his mid-nineties, he is still the managing director of his family's assets. Excerpts in this book came from his personal memoirs.

REBECCA SNIDER SPRECHER (contributor and co-editor) hails from Hopkinsville, Kentucky, and graduated from the University of North Carolina at Chapel Hill with a BA in communications. Two weeks later she was in Miami training to become a Pan American stewardess. Initially based in New York, she transferred to Honolulu, where she flew for six years. After leaving Pan Am, she worked for Xerox for ten years in Honolulu, later becoming a community volunteer on Oahu. In 2011, Becky published *Flying: A Novel*, co-written with fellow flight attendant Paula Helfrich. The book traces the high-speed lives of Pan Am crews in the Pacific during the 1970s. Since *Flying*'s publication, Becky has devoted countless hours of research toward preserving Pan Am's history. As a result, she has become an invited guest speaker at prestigious universities, Pan Am reunions, and various philanthropic organizations. Becky and her husband reside in Beaufort, South Carolina.

DIAN STIRN GROH (contributor and co-editor) grew up in the Midwest and graduated with a BA in sociology from Miami University, Oxford, Ohio. After flying as passenger on a Pan Am charter to Europe during college, she joined Pan Am as a stewardess. During her seventeen years with the airline, Dian became a purser, recruiter, flight attendant instructor, and grooming coordinator. She was based in Miami, New York, Honolulu, and Los Angeles. Post Pan Am, she became a professor and private tutor of ESL (English as a second language). She currently freelances nonfiction articles, short stories, and poetry. As the mother of twins, she has written for several lifestyle publications. Dian's first picture book, *My Maumee*, a history of her Ohio hometown, was published for her fiftieth class reunion. Dian resides near her children and grandchildren in Texas.

 JAMES TRAUTMAN (contributor) grew up in the early 1950s in the shadow of New Jersey's Newark Airport. He has maintained a lifelong love of aviation history and is a regular contributor to North American magazines, newspapers, radio, and television. His book *The Pan American Clippers: The Golden Age of Flying Boats*, is in its second printing. In June 2015, he was granted a full day's tour of Edwards Air Force Base and the NASA Neil Armstrong Research Facility in conjunction with his new book on the early test pilots and the X Planes. He resides in southern Ontario.

 MARGARET O'SHAUGHNESSY (contributor) was the organizer and hostess of the 2016 Pan Am Irish Spring Reunion. She is a native of Foynes, Ireland, which was the European crossroads of flying boat aviation from 1937 to 1945, and Ireland's first transatlantic airport. Along with avid aviation supporters, she opened the Flying Boat Museum on July 8, 1989. Today, as the museum's director and curator, Margaret employs twenty-five people who welcome 60,000 visitors a year. Margaret has compiled and edited the extremely popular *Foynes Museum Book* and has written numerous articles about the flying boats for newspapers and travel and tourism magazines. In addition, she has advised and researched for television documentaries. She has devoted the past twenty-five years to gathering flying boat memorabilia.

P an American. Unlike any other airline, past or present, the name evokes style, glamour, romance, adventure, innovation, daring feats, and heroism.

Pan Am was the airline that forever changed the world by pioneering impossible commercial routes across two great oceans. Pan Am established bases at distant Pacific atolls, opened routes to the Caribbean, Central and South America, and provided scheduled flights to eighty-one countries on six continents. Since 1935, Pan Am was covertly or overtly involved in supporting numerous US military operations, including WWII, the Cold War, Korea, and Vietnam. Pan Am set the gold standard for safety, first-class cuisine, and luxurious amenities, both on board and at their splendid Art Deco terminals. Moreover, Pan Am's contributions to aviation technology drastically changed the way we travel—then and now.

More than a quarter-century since the demise of Pan Am, people stop me in parking lots when they see the blue globe on my car's bumper sticker, or when they spot the logo on the purse I carry. Many of these people weren't yet born when Pan Am went bankrupt in 1991, yet they're familiar with the name, or have heard some of the incredible stories—the stuff of legends.

People of almost any age who grew up in Hawaii, as I did, light up when I proudly confirm I was one of the lucky stewardesses who flew for Pan Am. Admiring reactions hint at what celebrity must be like. Passengers flying Pan Am to or from Hawaii, as well as other destinations in the 1960s, were given navy-blue tote bags emblazoned with the blue-and-white Pan Am logo. The totes became part of a ubiquitous and unlikely island tradition when they quickly evolved into school bookbags. As if laying claim to a valuable artifact, I smile each time someone tells me about their Pan Am school bag. Often, the person will say, "I carried that bag all the way through high school, and you know what? I think I've still got it . . . somewhere."

Whether it's the "wing and globe"(1927 to 1956) or the more widely known "single globe" (1957 to 1991), Pan Am logos are still as universally recognized as Coca-Cola or Apple.

It's the same everywhere I go; sitting at a seaside bar in Pago Pago; riding a San Francisco streetcar; going through security check at the entrance to the Taj Mahal; checking in for a commuter flight in Grand Junction, Colorado; or when first meeting fellow travelers on a Botswana safari. Almost anywhere in the world, everyday folks hear the mention of Pan Am, or catch a glimpse of the logo, and strangers are drawn into conversation about the most iconic airline that ever flew.

Pan American Airways logo circa 1935. Courtesy Pan Am Historical Foundation (PAHF).

As the airline that always led the way, it was Pan Am founder Juan Trippe who pushed Boeing to build the B-707. Along with thousands of spectators at Seattle's annual Seafair festival, Boeing president Bill Allen and many other airline executives watched from the shore as ace test pilot "Tex" Johnson performed not one, but two breathtaking barrel-roll demonstrations of the 707 prototype, 400 feet over the lake. Two months later, Pan Am ordered a fleet of twenty. Airlines from all over the world soon followed Pan Am's lead, and the jet age was born.

But it was the innovative flying boats that Pan Am flew from 1929 to 1946, that ushered the airline into the early annals of aviation history. The large commercial "boats" flew for just over ten years before land planes and runways rendered them obsolete, but during that brief heyday, their impact on all aspects of aviation was as dramatically groundbreaking as man's later race to space.

The astounding feats of *China Clipper* and *Pacific Clipper* are as mythical as the mysterious disappearance of *Hawaii Clipper*. Each of Pan Am's twenty-eight flying boats has its own fascinating story, as did the crews and passengers who flew them. This anthology's generous and talented contributors (former Pan Am employees or those possessed with Pan Am "passion") will engage you in some never-before-told stories through their unique, individual "voices."

While there's little doubt about Pan American's singular role in aviation, another intangible element separates it from all other airlines—from nearly all other companies, airline or not.

Newsweek once described it as a "living, breathing soul." Whether the magazine's author knew it or not, they were referring to something only Pan Am employees could know and embrace. Pure and simple, it's an indelible loyalty springing forth from the company's historical beginnings, richly seasoned with personal experiences that have been shared and passed down from generation to generation.

Even though the average age of still-living former Pan Am employees is now over seventy, that "living, breathing soul" flourishes in both small and large ways. Whether it's two stewardesses recalling the harrowing last flight out of Saigon; a small, private gathering of the legendary Internal German Service Berlin-based crews; hundreds of flight attendants reveling at an International World Wings convention; or grand, all-inclusive reunions celebrated in the fashion befitting Pan Am's first-class reputation, working for Pan Am was, and still is, equivalent to membership in an exclusive, private club.

Irish Spring Reunion, Foynes, Ireland. Courtesy of Teresa Webber.

It is precisely this phenomenon of specialness and ongoing reunions that inspired the collective efforts of this book.

When we realized the 2016 location of a come-one-come-all Pan Am reunion would take place in Foynes, Ireland, we began thinking about the flying boats. Foynes was once strategically important for flying boat crossings between the US and Europe, just as Honolulu had been in the Pacific. None of Pan Am's flying boats have survived, but today the Foynes Flying Boat Museum houses the world's one and only full-sized replica of a grandiose Boeing 314, minus its wings. The mockup of *Yankee Clipper*'s fuselage, flight deck, and passenger cabins have been recreated with such attention to detail, it's like stepping back in time.

In 2012, at the invitation of His Serene Highness Prince Albert II, the *Dixie Clipper* Reunion took place in the sparkling principality of Monaco. Under the organization of Captain Don Cooper and Max Gurney, former district sales manager for southern France and personal friend of the Royal Family, 550 Pan Am employees from across the globe gathered to celebrate the first 1938 transatlantic passenger crossing from Port Washington, Long Island, to Marseilles flown on *Dixie Clipper*.

Dixie Clipper Reunion, Monaco. Courtesy of Mary Lou Bigelow, former Pan Am stewardess/purser.

Not to be outdone, two years later, in April 2014, again with Captain Cooper at the helm, a banner hanging over the seaside entrance of the Waikiki Prince Hotel welcomed 500 former Pan Am employees and their guests to the Aloha Reunion. Hawaii was a long distance for most to travel, but the idea of a reunion in "paradise" was embraced with enthusiasm and excitement. Since the beginnings of the flying boats, virtually all of Pan Am's long-range aircraft and crews had laid over amid the balmy climes of Honolulu.

It was during the Irish Spring Foynes Reunion that Captain Cooper announced he would not organize any further events. "I'm too damn old," he protested, but his fellow legendary Berlin-based pilots, self-dubbed the "Black Sheep," demanded another, very special gathering. Post WWII, they had flown thousands of Internal German Service (IGS) flights under the banner of Pan American. Often contrary to the mother company's policies, the Black Sheep operated according to their own fly gods. Don agreed, and this time more than 500 Pan Amers and their guests would gather in Berlin in May of 2017.

Many excellent books have been published about Pan Am's remarkable era of flying boats, some penned by authors presented in this book, but we all agreed a fresh historical telling, as well as rarely documented personal stories told by still-living crewmembers and passengers, were important and necessary.

Through our combined research, firsthand knowledge, and personal experiences, we hope *Hunting the Wind* will take you on a fascinating, enlightening journey back in time to one of aviation's most exciting eras.

Fasten your seatbelt, and welcome on board!

Pan Am Boeing 727s of the Internal German Service at Flughafen Tempelhof, West Berlin, West Germany. *Courtesy of PAHF.*

Internal German Service (IGS)

After WWII, Germany was divided into four zones between the three victorious Western Allies (Britain, France, and the USA), as well as the Soviet Union (USSR). The quadripartite powers prohibited German owned or run air service, but the need for both internal and international transportation was acute to restoring a devastated Germany. Due to rising Cold War tensions, the USSR withdrew from the Allied Control Commission in 1948, and began plans to build a dividing wall between East and West Berlin (initiated in 1961). Per a 1954 agreement between the three Western Allies, Pan American inaugurated their Internal German Service (IGS) with an already existing hub in Berlin, and a technical base in Frankfurt. For nearly forty years, more passengers boarded Pan Am flights at Berlin's historic Tempelhof airport than at most all other airports in the world. From the beginning, the short-hauling IGS operated on many levels like a separate entity from the mother company. IGS employed hundreds of German

Pan Am flag flies outside Pan Am Berlin Reunion, spring 2017. *Courtesy of Rebecca Sprecher*

citizens, including flight attendants, but only a select handful of US cockpit crews. The still-legendary, affable, and independent-minded IGS pilots appropriately called themselves the Black Sheep. Starting with DC-4s, the fleet eventually grew to an all-jet operation of Boeing 727s, but with German reunification in 1989, the role of IGS became superfluous. In 1990, IGS was taken over by the German carrier Lufthansa. Soon thereafter, IGS pilots were integrated into Pan Am's international "blue water" routes. (Information provided by PAHF, Don Cooper, and Wikipedia).

In The Beginning

Teresa Webber
and Jamie Dodson

CHAPTER I

*I*t was a balmy late afternoon on October 18, 1927, in the Florida Keys. Standing on the float, the mechanic made one last check inside the engine to be sure the oil leak was sealed. Then he gave a thumbs-up to the pilot. Cy Caldwell took the last bite of his stale sandwich and walked toward the precarious-looking flying machine.

"Okay Jim, let's fuel up so I can get to Haiti before dark."

"Sure thing, Cy," he replied.

Jim fueled and fixed airplanes for a living, but he wouldn't be caught dead flying in one. This plane, like most, was made of nothing more than canvas fabric held together by a flimsy wooden frame. Even more dangerous, it ran on highly flammable automobile gasoline. *Nobody* traveled on airplanes, especially not over water. Everyone knew the new-fangled airplanes were just a novelty. They would never be of any practical use. Besides, they just weren't safe.

The mechanic shook his head. He figured Cy had some kind of death wish or else he was just plain crazy. Damn near as crazy as Charles Lindbergh, who, six months before, somehow flew solo across the Atlantic from New York to Paris in a single-engine landplane.

Jim knew that Cy taught himself to fly when he was only a kid, then flew as an exhibition pilot before enlisting with the Canadian Flying Corps in WWI. After returning to his native Canada, Cy transported Royal Mounties and Forest Reserve officers into remote wilderness outposts. Later, for the Canadian Navy, he tested torpedo-carrying planes. Dangerous work.

Yup, no doubt about it. Cy Caldwell was nutty as a fruitcake. The Fairchild FC-2 floatplane, *La Nina*, was gassed and ready to go when a voice called out from the nearby office of Aeromarine Airways.

"Phone call, Cy. Long distance. Must be important."

"Who is it?"

"Someone named Whitbeck. Says he's the Key West station manager for a new airline. He's calling on behalf of the head honcho."

Cy was just strapping in, but he climbed out of the cockpit and walked toward the Aeromarine office. "Never heard of him," he said, picking up the telephone's earpiece. Then, speaking into the horn, "Caldwell here."

"Mister Caldwell," the voice crackled. "My name is E. J. Whitbeck. I represent Juan Trippe and Pan American Systems."

"Who?"

"I'll cut to the chase, Mister Caldwell. We urgently need you and your plane."

"When?"

"Tomorrow morning."

"No can do, Mister Whitbeck. It's not my plane, and I'm scheduled to fly out of here right now to Haiti."

"This is very important, Mister Caldwell."

"Yeah? So's my job. You flying contraband or what?"

"Mail," Whitbeck replied.

"Mail?"

"Yes, United States mail. If it doesn't reach Havana by tomorrow, Pan American will lose the first government airmail contract, and we'll go bankrupt."

Wishing he'd taken off before the call came in, Cy mustered his limited patience for corporate nonsense. "Sorry, Mister Whitbeck. Not my problem. Like I said, it's not my plane, and I have a flight plan."

"Would $250 be enough to borrow the plane and change your route?"

Cy paused. "That's a lot of money."

"It's yours for an hour flight to Havana. Then you can continue on to Haiti. No one will be the wiser, but I need an answer now."

At 0700 hours the next morning, on October 19, 1927, seven bags of US mail (about 30,000 letters) were loaded onto *La Nina*. Sixty-two minutes later, after setting down at Havana, Cuba, reluctant pilot Cy Caldwell changed the course of aviation history by changing his mind.

Two years later, the stock market crashed, plunging America and most of the world into the Great Depression (1929–39). Millions of investors were wiped out, and nearly half of US banks closed. When the Depression reached its disastrous peak in 1933, the total US population was less than 126 million with an unemployment rate of twenty-five percent. No emergency relief programs were in place until the Roosevelt administration enacted a series of bills known as the New Deal (1933–38). Along with numerous reforms, one of the prime targets was to bring about immediate economic

Pan Am Flying Boat Firsts

Compiled by John Steele
Pan Am Historical Foundation

1929
- First airline to develop and use instrument flight techniques
- First American airline to employ cabin attendants and serve meals aloft
- First American airline to develop a complete aviation weather service

1930
- First American airline to offer international air express service

— 1925 — 1926 — 1927 — 1928 — 1929 — 1930 — 1931 — 1932 — 1933 — 1934 — 1

1928
- First American airline to use radio communications
- First American airline to carry emergency lifesaving equipment
- First American airline to use multiple flight crews

- First American airline to develop an airport and airways traffic control system
- First American airline to order and purchase aircraft built to its own specifications (Sikorsky S-38)

1931
- First American airline to develop and operate four-engine flying boats

relief. However, in the despairing interim, farms failed, migrant workers wandered in search of work, untold numbers went homeless, daily unemployment lines stretched many city blocks, food rationing became a daily necessity, soup kitchens and bread lines sprang up, and an overwhelming sense of hopelessness prevailed.

It couldn't have been a worse time to start a business, especially not in the suspicious, unchartered field of commercial aviation. It was an unreceptive time for new ideas and new beginnings. By all sane and logical accounts, wading into the murky waters of aviation was a very bad idea—bad, unless your name was Juan Terry Trippe.

Stubbornness, intrepidness, a deep-rooted spirit of competition, dogged negotiating skills, and vision; these characteristics would guide young entrepreneur Juan Trippe toward his ultimate goals—global air routes, and making air travel affordable to the "everyman." His prophetic vision propelled the budding airline to the forefront of aviation, leading the airline industry into the flying boat era, the jet age, and eventually to the creation of the first wide-body aircraft.

Juan Trippe.
Courtesy of
PAHF.

1932
First airline to sell all-expense international air tours

1939
First airline to operate scheduled transatlantic passenger and mail service

1943
First commercial American airline to carry a sitting US president—Franklin Roosevelt from Miami to Casablanca

6 — 1937 — 1938 — 1939 — 1940 — 1941 — 1942 — 1943 — 1944 — 1945 — 1946 —

1935
First airline to develop and employ long-range weather forecasting

First airline to operate scheduled transpacific passenger and mail service

First American airline to install facilities for heating food aboard an aircraft

1942
First airline to complete a round-the-world flight

First airline to operate international service with all-cargo aircraft

1944
First airline to propose a plan for low-cost, mass transportation on a worldwide basis

Following Cy Caldwell's 1927 delivery of US airmail from Key West to Havana, the first scheduled passenger flight took place six days later on a Fokker F-7 landplane, flying the same route.

Small planes were soon replaced by larger, long-range models, and in the early 1930s, Pan Am's fleet expanded to include the newer, bigger, and faster Sikorsky flying boats. From bases in Miami, Florida; and Brownsville, Texas; Pan Am grew to encircle the Caribbean, eventually servicing every major Latin American city.

Next in Trippe's sights were Atlantic routes to Europe, plus unimagined Pacific routes to the Orient. His single-minded focus and relentless negotiating skills marked an aviation milestone when he hired the world-renowned, highly sought-after Charles Lindbergh and his copilot/wife, Anne Morrow. The Lindberghs' mission was to conduct survey flights of an unexplored northern route to China, as well as an alternative route across the uncharted Pacific. After both dangerous surveys were completed, Charles and Anne reported that any and all routes would require aircraft not yet conceived, let alone built. True to his nature, Trippe did not regard this as a stumbling stone. All he needed were bigger, better aircraft designs.

When the astounding concept of air travel, especially across the Atlantic and Pacific, was first offered to passengers, well-heeled travelers were accustomed to the comforts of ocean liners. Moreover, they were leery of the new flying machines. To counterbalance the perception of danger and lack of luxuries, Trippe named his airplanes "Clippers," subliminally referring to his ocean liner competitors, American, Cunard, and Matson Lines.

It was a brilliant decision. By 1935, flying boats had reached a level of awe and international fame, most notably when the *China Clipper* made her sensational departure from San Francisco en route to Manila with layover stops in Honolulu, Midway, Wake, and Guam. Under the command of veteran pilot Captain Edward Musick, the splendid Martin M-130 crossed the vast Pacific Ocean in only six-and-a-half days. By a fast passenger ship, it took three weeks. Following *China Clipper*'s phenomenal feat, the public elevated Captain Musick to the hero status of his contemporary, Charles Lindbergh, or, by today's measure, astronaut Neil Armstrong. Pan American had become a household word.

By the late 1930s, Trippe's escalating airline had made impressive strides with scheduled flights covering South America and the Caribbean. By then, Pan Am had paved the way to Asia across the Pacific with plans to begin 1939 transatlantic flights from the US to Europe. Meanwhile, Trippe's subsidiary airlines flew routes in China and Alaska.

Nevertheless, to feasibly carry cargo and passengers on long oceanic hauls, Trippe still needed non-existing aircraft with bigger, long-range capabilities. That was when he approached the airline manufacturing companies of Commodore, Sikorsky, Martin, and Boeing.

Pan Am's core team worked in concert with Boeing's designer, Wellwood Beall, ultimately resulting in the B-314. The massive double-decker airplane was like nothing anyone had seen before. Among other unique features, Beall's plans incorporated the enormous wing of a cancelled XB-15 bomber with four 2,000-horsepower Wright Whirlwind engines. When the B-314 made its San Francisco debut in 1938, the world was agog. Like the 747 "Jumbo Jet," and the monstrous Airbus A-380, the B-314 was the largest, most mind-boggling passenger plane of its day.

By 1938, the Great Depression was coming to an end, but its devastating effects still lingered. In the hearts and minds of millions, the technically groundbreaking B-314s, fitted with every passenger comfort, reignited glamour and romance reminiscent of the carefree Roaring Twenties. Across the board, the B-314 Clippers made a huge impact on commercial advertising, films, books, and music, delivering intoxicating notions of excitement and hope. Overnight, people from all walks of life could imagine themselves emerging from desperate times, escaping to distant, exotic lands on board the most luxurious flying machine ever built.

The Great Depression be damned! Pan American's flying boats made everything seem possible—a glimpse into a hopeful future.

At $1,400 for a round-trip ticket between San Francisco and Manila (a lot of money at the time), only high-ranking military officers, aristocrats, heads of state, and the rich and famous could afford passage on the 314 Clippers, but the very idea of a five-star airborne "hotel," replete with gourmet dining, lounges, sleeping berths—even a bridal suite—conjured wondrous fantasies of high-class travel, style, and exotic destinations.

Decades before Pan American emerged as history's most iconic and innovative airline, Juan Trippe owned or ran no less than a dozen other airline companies. But were it not for his vision and persistence, one daredevil Canadian pilot, a select group of handpicked advisers and aviators, loyal employees, financial backers, and the companies who built his airplanes, it's anyone's guess as to what course aviation might have taken.

In an era when the public regarded air travel as nothing more than a dangerous passing fad, single-minded visionary Trippe proved them wrong. From the 1927 single-engine seaplane *La Nina* to the Commodore, Sikorsky, Martin, and Boeing flying boats—and on into the jet age—even now, three decades since its demise, the legendary saga of Pan American Airways continues to endure.

Introducing Pan Am's Flying Boats

Sikorsky S-38

It was the twin-engine, two-crew, ten-passenger amphibian S-38 that launched the early commercial successes of Juan Trippe and aircraft manufacturer Igor Sikorsky. Born in 1889 in Kiev, Russia (now Ukraine), the aeronautics engineer immigrated to the United States in 1919, becoming a US citizen in 1928. In 1925, in partnership with former Russian military officers, he formed the Sikorsky Manufacturing Company, located near Roosevelt Field on Long Island. Later, he built a plant at Bridgeport, Connecticut. In 1929 his company became a division of United Aircraft Corporation, based in Stratford, Connecticut. Pan American eventually acquired the entire fleet of thirty-eight Sikorsky-built S-38s, developed from the earlier S-34 and S-36 models, and flew them extensively throughout the Caribbean and Central America. Charles and Anne Lindbergh flew the S-38 on survey flights for Pan Am in South America and the Pacific. Regarded by many as a genius, Sikorsky would become

S-38 at Dinner Key. *Courtesy of PAHF.*

known for creating the first four-engine commercial airplane, the S-40. However, his most notable aviation achievement may be the creation of the world's first working helicopter, the S-47.

Consolidated Commodore

Along with the Sikorsky S-38, Pan Am started its Caribbean and Central and South American routes with the Consolidated Commodores. They were the first American-built large commercial flying boats. In 1929, Consolidated Aircraft bid on a US Navy contract to build a long-range model that could fly nonstop between the US mainland, Panama, Alaska, and Hawaii. They lost the bid to the Glenn L. Martin Company, but soon offered a commercial flying boat version, known as the Commodore. Through one of its subsidiaries, New York Rio Buenos Aires Airline (NYRBA), Pan Am acquired and flew all fourteen of the Commodores. In terms of luxurious furnishings, large passenger windows, and even a lavatory, they came close to measuring up to Trippe's interior design requirements. Close, but the Commodores fell short filling the whole bill. With a one-hundred-foot wingspan, the two-engine, all-metal flying boat could accommodate thirty-two passengers and a three-man crew on short segments. However, on long hauls of about 1,000 miles, it could carry no more than fourteen, including the crew. Although the Commodore was an important design step in the development of flying boat monoplanes (most notably the 1936 Consolidated PBY Catalina), Trippe and his close advisers leaned heavily toward Sikorsky, Martin, and Boeing.

Consolidated Commodore landing on Biscayne Bay, Florida. *Courtesy of PAHF.*

Sikorsky S-40

Named after his Cuban step-grandfather, Juan Pedro Terry, the up-and-coming aviation mogul was a meticulous man. Nothing Juan Terry Trippe ever did was by accident, which was evident in 1931, when he trademarked his airplanes Clippers. The first aircraft Trippe dubbed a Clipper was a Sikorsky S-40. He may have chosen the name *American Clipper* in patriotism to his country, as well as in association with the East Indies tea trade of the 1860s, when sleek, rakish clipper ships plied the seas.

In the years before the Clippers, the growing airline flew an assortment of venerable aircraft: the Sikorsky S-38 amphibians, Ford Tri-motors, Consolidated Commodore flying boats, Fokker Tri-motors, and a host of other aircraft from nearly every reputable manufacturer. Much of the fleet's oddball aircraft came from Trippe's acquisition of smaller, and often competing airlines.

The S-40 design was essentially an up-scaled S-38. However, while the S-38 carried eight to ten passengers in Spartan-like accommodations, the S-40 could carry thirty-eight passengers in Pullman car luxury. At that time, it was the largest plane to fly in passenger service. At 115 mph, it was slow by today's standards, but it could go where no train could go, and at twice the average speed.

On October 10, 1931, Pan Am Chief Pilot Basil Rowe flew the yet unnamed S-40 flying boat from Sikorsky's Bridgeport factory to Anacostia, Maryland, where First Lady Lou Hoover christened it the *American Clipper* with a bottle of Caribbean water. (No champagne because Prohibition was still in effect.) In his 1957 autobiography, *Under My Wings*, Captain Rowe proclaims the S-40 was "one of the best airplanes" he'd flown at that time.

One month later, November 19, 1931, on its first passenger flight, and under the command of Charles Lindbergh with Basil Rowe in the copilot seat, *American Clipper* made three stops between Miami and Cristobal in the Panama Canal Zone. In contrast to Captain Rowe's praise of the S-40, Lindbergh described it as a "flying forest" because of its exposed struts and wires, which created drag, thereby limiting speed, range, and fuel efficiency. It was, however, the S-40 that pioneered Pan Am's maritime theme, not only with the name Clipper but also with crew uniforms designed to resemble US naval officers, as well as the use of maritime terminology. Future airlines would follow Pan Am's lead, using the same maritime terms such as cockpit, port, starboard, galleys, bulkheads, and the ranks of crewmembers—captain, first officer, engineer, purser, and steward.

Sikorsky delivered only three S-40s to Pan Am—the *American Clipper, Caribbean Clipper*, and *Southern Clipper*. The S-40 was a step in the right direction, but Trippe and his trusted adviser, Charles Lindbergh, were far from convinced it was the ultimate answer to all of Pan Am's needs. At the same time the three S-40s were beginning their Pan Am careers, Trippe and Lindbergh turned again to Igor Sikorsky, asking him to design a larger, more efficient model.

According to Robert Daley in *An American Saga: Juan Trippe and His Pan Am Empire*, it was during that first passenger flight on November 19, 1931, when Captain Lindbergh turned the controls over to Basil Rowe and went aft to sit next to the most important passenger on board, Igor Sikorsky. Lindbergh explained that what he and Trippe wanted was a really new airplane, something completely clean in design, with no external bracing, no outriggers, no fuselage hanging from the wing by struts, "no engines stuffed amid the struts like wine bottles in a rack." Sikorsky countered, saying that what they wanted was "two steps ahead in development." Sikorsky wanted to take it one step at a time; lives were at stake with no margins for mistakes. Lindbergh made a sketch on the back of the flight's menu. Sikorsky considered it. Later that evening, in a Jamaican hotel, the two men worked it out, and the S-42 was conceived.

Sikorsky S-42

Commissioned by Trippe for Pan Am's intended Atlantic routes, the S-42 was a magnificent leap in aviation technology. But much to Trippe's frustration, by 1934 it became evident the British, who controlled all destination refueling stops, would not grant Pan American landing rights at any of Great Britain's ports of call. The issues were matters of British politics as well as national pride, especially since the Brits were unable to produce anything close to the advanced S-42.

Sikorsky's design incorporated a wing that could carry double the load of every existing airplane. He solved the wings' high takeoff and landing speed requirements with an innovative tailing edge flap, the first to be installed on a production aircraft. Another "first" in commercial aviation was embedding the engines in wing nacelles. Considered risky, the design reduced drag, allowing greater speed and range. In the days before propeller feathering, if an engine quit in flight, the wind-milling prop created huge drag, whereby the wing area behind lost lift. However, Sikorsky trusted in the increasing

viability of Pratt & Whitney's engines. Relying on Pratt & Whitney, his S-42 innovations set an industry standard. The result was a state-of-the-art engineering marvel—an aircraft able to span the Atlantic with far fewer refueling stops every 1,200 miles.

Robert Daley, in *An American Saga*, noted that in mid-1934 Trippe had three S-42s on hand, as well as three Martin M-130s on order, but with no place to fly them. Two S-42s went into Latin American service, and one was returned to Sikorsky for modification. Sikorsky upgraded the engines and installed eight huge fuel tanks in gutted passenger compartments. The revised S-42A had a range of 2,500 miles—double that of her two Latin American sisters. However, the newly christened *Pan American Clipper* was unable to carry passengers. She would hence become a survey ship for many years, pioneering flights across the Pacific to Hawaii, Midway, and Wake. Later, chief pilot Ed Musick would fly the modified S-42A south to American Samoa and New Zealand.

Martin M-130

The Martin M-130 was a commercial flying boat designed and built for Pan American in 1935, by the Glenn L. Martin Company in Baltimore, Maryland. Glenn Martin called the craft the Martin Ocean Transports, but to the public they were known as the "China Clippers," a generic name for Pan Am's large flying boats. Three were built: the *China Clipper*, the *Philippine Clipper*, and the *Hawaii Clipper*.

On November 22, 1935, the *China Clipper*, piloted by Captain Edwin C. Musick and First Officer R.O.D. Sullivan, flew the first

transpacific airmail route. Weekly passenger flights across the Pacific began in October 1936, when *Hawaii Clipper* left San Francisco for Manila, laying over at Honolulu, Midway, Wake, and Guam.

In a bid for the next round of Pan Am flying boats, Martin built a fourth Martin Ocean Transport, the M-156. It was similar to the M-130, but had a larger wing, giving it greater range, plus twin vertical stabilizers. Trippe chose the larger, technologically superior Boeing B-314. As a result, Martin sold the M-156 to the USSR. Referred to as the *Russian Clipper*, it flew for Aeroflot until it crashed in 1948 off the Kamchatka Peninsula.

By 1941, only Martin's *China* and *Philippine Clipper*s remained in service with Pan Am. *Hawaii Clipper* mysteriously vanished without a trace in August 1938 between Guam and Manila. After the Japanese attack on Pearl Harbor (December 7, 1941), the *China Clipper* and other Pan Am Clippers mustered aircraft, pilots, and ground crews to help win WWII in the Pacific. Only a few years later, *China Clipper* would become a top-secret agent for the OSS (later known as the CIA).

China Clipper went on to play a strategic role in securing Pan Am's global fame. Theoretical physicist Albert Einstein was worried that Nazi Germany would seize uranium from mines in Czechoslovakia and develop an atomic bomb. In a letter to Franklin Roosevelt, he urged the president to obtain a supply of uranium from a different source and secretly transport it to the United States for what would become known as the atom bomb-building Manhattan Project.

The Shinkolobwe mine in the Belgian Congo (now the Democratic Republic of the Congo) produced the richest uranium ore in the world. President Roosevelt took Einstein's advice. In deep secrecy from Pan Am's service base at Leopoldville, Belgian Congo, the *China Clipper* flew tons of Shinkolobwe uranium ($200 million in annual orders) to the United States.

Boeing 314

The Boeing Airplane Company produced the grandest flying boats of the time. Employing the massive wing of Boeing's earlier XB-15 bomber prototype, it achieved the necessary range to cross the Atlantic and Pacific Oceans, and in many other ways, far exceeded its flying boat predecessors. Commercially, it was able to carry high-grossing cargo with the greatest numbers of passengers who were pampered in decadence akin to the most posh hotels in the world.

Only twelve B-314s were built. Trippe sold three to Imperial Airways, later to become the British Overseas Airways Corporation (BOAC). The other nine were brought into Pan Am's well-established commercial routes. The fabulous Boeing 314 had a cruising speed of 188 miles per hour, shaving off time on long transoceanic flights. On long hauls such as the nineteen-hour flight from San Francisco to Honolulu, Pan Am reduced passenger capacity from seventy-four to thirty-six to provide a sleeping berth for each passenger. On shorter flights, passengers were also pampered in ways never before seen in the airline industry.

Prior to the onset of WWII, Pan Am's Boeing Clippers were the epitome of one-class deluxe travel. But Clipper rates didn't come at bargain prices. The one-way fare between New York and Southampton was $685 ($11,505 in today's dollars). Round-trip between San Francisco and Hong Kong via the "stepping-stone" islands of Oahu, Midway, Wake, and Guam was $1,368 ($23,350 in today's dollars). In other words, Trippe's goal of making air travel affordable to the "everyman" still loomed in the future.

The 1941 Japanese attack on Pearl Harbor changed everything across the globe. For one, it brought Pan American directly into WWII as an active player. Amid the dearth of aircraft, trained pilots, navigators, radio operators, engineers, and ground equipment, the US military was unprepared to fight the Japanese in the Pacific, but true to his ever-prevailing sense of patriotic duty, Trippe transferred his magnificent B-314s to the US Navy. At the onset of WWII, Pan Am operated the world's only transoceanic air system, including the best-trained and most experienced pilots, plus ground staff and infrastructure to support operations. The bombing of Pearl Harbor made prey of Pan Am's strategic Pacific bases. The Clippers themselves became enemy targets all around the globe.

Pan Am came to the rescue of the United States over and over again in all senses: militarily, economically, and in terms of boosting the American spirit.

Transatlantic passenger flights to neutral Portugal and Ireland continued after war broke out in Europe in September 1939, and remained in service until 1945.

During their brief eleven-year careers, 314 Clippers laid milestones in aviation technology, safety standards, and passenger service. They brought exotic destinations within reach of air travelers and represented the romance of flight. On December 7, 1941, they began playing an indispensable role in the course of WWII. Often overlooked in the annals of history, Pan American's Boeing 314 Clippers were essential in taking America and its allies to victory.

CHAPTER 2

We are the dreamers of dreams—the movers and shakers of the world.
—Arthur O'Shaughnessy (1844–1881)

V isionary Pan American founder Juan Terry Trippe was the first aviation tycoon in history, but his personality and leadership style didn't fit the prevailing image of successful global CEOs. Alec Baldwin's portrayal of Trippe as a verbose corporate bully in *The Aviator* was the antithesis of the real Trippe. Rather than making demands, Trippe calmly made suggestions—suggestions that everyone who worked for Pan Am took seriously. He never swore, seldom raised his voice, and displayed little or no emotion, even when confronted with frustrating challenges. If he didn't get his way when dealing with business associates, he simply persisted until they gave in. In his personal and business life, he could be effusively charming or distantly cool. Robert Daley, author of *An American Saga: Juan Trippe and His Pan Am Empire,* describes his subject as quiet and undramatic, yet stubborn and tenacious, "as much a daredevil as any of the bullfighters or racing drivers I had known."

Juan T Trippe.
Courtesy of PAHF.

Adding to the complexities of Trippe's nature are personal accounts by Betty Stettinius, his wife for fifty-three years and author of *Pan Am's First Lady.* Also documented are rare interviews with youngest son Edward Trippe, chairman of the Pan Am Historical Foundation, and Kathleen Clair, Trippe's indispensible private secretary for thirty-two years. According to those closest to him, the otherwise enigmatic Trippe was a loyal husband, a dedicated father, and a considerate boss.

It's been written over and over again that Trippe spent his life pursuing a "dream." Some say it was one of world domination by air; others claim it was to bring affordable air travel to the average man; still others theorize it was to shrink the world, thereby uniting people across the globe with a better understanding of each other.

Altruistic or not, Trippe's "dream" was not spurred by ego or his lust for personal glory and fame. Like his friends Charles Lindbergh and Ed Musick, Trippe was introspective to the point of shyness and secretiveness. The three giants of aviation avoided media attention at all costs, seldom revealing closely guarded personal details of their lives.

Just as US presidents appoint cabinet members, Trippe surrounded himself with a highly skilled team of people who were key to Pan Am's success, each one trustworthy and gifted in their fields of expertise.

L TO R: CAPT. EDWIN MUSICK, ANDRE PRIESTER, VP ENGINEERING, COL. CHARLES A. LINDBERGH, JUAN T. TRIPPE, IGOR SIKORSKY, 2 NEWSMEN 1930s

Charles Lindbergh was perhaps the most heralded hero of the twentieth century. He and his wife, copilot, navigator, radio operator, and author, Anne Morrow Lindbergh, overcame extraordinary odds when surveying Pan Am's early routes, thereby establishing most of Pan Am's worldwide structures.

Pan Am's board of directors rewarded Charles with a seat on the board, plus the position of technical adviser. More importantly, he became Trippe's close friend and personal adviser.

Sikorsky S-42 roll-out, Stratford, Connecticut, *Courtesy of PAHF*

Lindberghs and Trippes standing in front of an early S-38. *Courtesy of PAHF.*

Anne carved her own place in history, not only as her husband's "wing-woman," but also by excelling as a photographer and author of two dozen books, notably *Hour of Gold, Hour of Lead: Diaries and Letters, 1929–1932* and *North to the Orient.*

Charles and Anne met in Mexico City in 1927, where her father was the US ambassador; they married two years later. During the next few years, their extraordinary pioneering adventures opened new routes and spurred the development of revolutionary aircraft for Pan Am. Charles and Anne Lindbergh were *the* couple of the century, but in 1932, tragedy struck when their first-born son, Charles Jr., was kidnapped and eventually murdered. Overwhelmed with grief and an unrelenting media, they exiled themselves to England for several years.

André Allart Priester, one of the company's most influential men was Pan Am's first-hired pioneer. Trippe appointed him vice president, chief engineer, and manager of operations to oversee most of the airline's early startup operations. The headstrong Dutchman standardized company procedures system-wide, including uncompromising regulations for employee conduct, as well as safety designs for the Boeing 314. Among many other contributions to Pan Am's early beginnings, he also brought invaluable movers and shakers to Trippe's "cabinet." (For more on Priester, see chapter 5.)

Andre Allart Priester. *Courtesy of PAHF.*

Hugo Leuteritz, credited by author, historian, and former Pan Am pilot Robert Gandt as a "radio wizard," invented the long-range direction finder, a revolutionary navigational device still used today.

Hired away from Radio Corporation of America (RCA) by Priester in 1928, young Leuteritz was already working on a compact, lightweight radio, one he knew would be practical for installation on airplanes. At the time, radio equipment was too heavy and cumbersome for airplanes. Besides that, the notion of radio navigation was untried and suspiciously regarded, especially by pilots. Even RCA viewed it as a ridiculous idea.

Ever since barely surviving a ditching between Havana and Key West, when the Fokker's pilot completely missed the coast of Florida, Leuteritz had understandably held a keenly personal interest in reliable radio navigation: a long-range direction finder.

Trippe fully understood that without precise navigational aids, it would be risky for his Clipper pilots to pinpoint the tiny island specks of Wake and Midway for their crossings of the vast Pacific en route to Asia. They were risks he couldn't afford to take.

At the time, flight crews were depending solely on antiquated celestial or unreliable dead reckoning navigation. (See chapter 5 for more on early navigation.) Trippe wholeheartedly welcomed Leuteritz to the startup team, and in 1935, he jubilantly informed Trippe that his long-range direction finder was finally working. It had taken him years of fine-tuning and many months of convincing pilots to use and trust radio navigation.

The last surviving Pan Am founding pioneer died at the age of ninety-five, leaving a remarkable legacy—one that virtually revolutionized aviation development.

Radio Engineer 'Hugo' Leuteritz. Courtesy of PAHF.

Samuel F. Pryor Jr. and his wife, Mary Tay, were close friends of Charles and Anne Lindbergh. Trippe appointed the exuberant Pryor to executive vice president in 1941 to act as Pan Am's indispensable political liaison to Congress. During WWII, under the guise of expanding Pan Am's passenger and mail routes, Pryor developed top-secret air corridors for military brass and American spies, and built fifty-six strategic military bases, which later served Pan Am commercially. For his service to aviation, President Truman awarded him the President's Medal for Merit in 1946.

Pryor's dedication to Pan Am and his larger-than-life personality came with unusual interests: his vast collection of 8,000 dolls from all over the world, plus his abiding passion for gibbon apes. To the astonishment of cabin crews, one of Sam's gibbons was sometimes seated next to him in first class on 707 or 747 Pan Am flights.

In 1965, Sam Pryor retired from Pan Am. He, Mary Tay, two of their five children, plus the family of pet gibbons, moved to the pristinely remote acreage they owned at Kipahulu, Maui. Pryor later gifted an adjoining five acres to the Lindberghs, where they too built a home for much-needed retreats. Sam and Charles spent much of their time preserving native plants on the acreage while Mary Tay whipped up delicious dishes for the two families' evening meals.

Sam Pryor Jr. Courtesy of the Sam Pryor Family.

Sam, Charles, Mary Tay, and four of the gibbons are buried at Kipahulu's Palapala Hoʻomau Church. After Anne's death in Vermont at the age of ninety-four, some of her ashes were scattered at various sites in Hawaii.

Pryor's books are *Make It Happen*, *My Interesting Life*, and *All God's Creatures*.

John Adams Hambleton, Cornelius Vanderbilt Whitney, and Juan Terry Trippe were three of the original founders of Pan American Airways. Similar to the Trippe family, the Hambletons were investment bankers with roots dating back nine generations to the Eastern Shore of Maryland. Like the younger Trippe, Hambleton was part of a brotherhood of young bankers and businessmen who flew their own airplanes. It was through this fraternity of privilege, plus a keen mutual interest in aviation, that the two men became close friends.

After graduating from Saint Paul's Preparatory Academy, Hambleton entered Harvard. One semester later, he dropped out and enlisted in the Army Signal Corps, flying harrowing WWI missions with the legendary 95th Aero Squadron. Major Hambleton returned home a decorated hero, laden in medals, including the Croix de Guerre and the Distinguished Service Cross with Oak Leaf Cluster.

When the war ended in 1918, Hambleton teamed up with buddies Trippe and Whitney to form Pan American Airways System in which he played key roles securing financing and government contracts.

In 1929, Capt. Charles Lindbergh and copilot John Hambleton flew Pan Am's first flight to Puerto Rico from Miami via Cuba, Haiti, and the Dominican Republic. Later that year, Hambleton captained a financial survey flight to Panama, setting up refueling stops in Central America for the first airmail flight from the US to the Canal Zone.

February 19, 1927, Charles Lindbergh (left) and John Hambelton (right) deliver the first airmail to the Panama Canal Zone from a Sikorski S-38 amphibian. *Courtesy of PAHF.*

The dashingly handsome Hambleton was rich and confident. Cut from the same cloth as Trippe, he and his friend dabbled in revolutionary ideas, including the bizarre notion of transoceanic polar flights. Because of their friendship, mutual respect, and shared visions for the future of Pan Am, Hambleton might have taken over when Trippe retired in 1968, but in June 1929, he broke a vow never to fly unless he was at the controls. At age thirty-one, Hambleton was killed in a private plane crash in Wilmington, North Carolina. He was a passenger.

John G. Borger's Pan Am career spanned forty-seven years, from flying boats to jumbo jets. "Borgie," as he was affectionately called, was key to the development and sustainment of many of Pan Am's iconic aircraft, including his participation in the design of Boeing's 314 flying boats. He graduated from the Massachusetts Institute of Technology in 1934 with a bachelor of science degree in aeronautical engineering, and Pan Am hired him the following January.

His first job was ordering half a million dollars in supplies and equipment for the company's soon-to-be-built Pacific bases. He sailed with the supplies on the first *SS North Haven* voyage and spent months on Wake Atoll overseeing placement and construction. (See chapter 3.)

In 1943, chief engineer André Priester recruited Borger to New York's engineering staff. Much later, in 1963, Borger replaced the retiring Priester, and in 1971, the Pan Am board of directors elected Borger vice president and chief engineer.

Borger could speak with technical acumen on every aspect of airliners—from seat design to engine thrust. By the end of the flying boat era, he was key to the introduction of the Lockheed L-049 Constellations, Boeing 377 Stratocruisers, and Douglas DC-6s and DC-7s.

In addition to his essential roles at Pacific bases on Wake and Midway, Borger is also known for championing Pan Am's daring move from propeller to turbojet propulsion, which eventually led to the jet age. Amid the constant turnover of corporate management, Borger was a steady, stabilizing influence for flight operations, maintenance, and engineering. He was an industry icon and a member of numerous prestigious aeronautical and engineering societies. In 2003, he was awarded the Guggenheim Medal for outstanding service to humanity.

John Borger, Wake Island, 1935. Courtesy of PAHF.

John A. Leslie was highly regarded by everyone at Pan Am, including Trippe. Soft-spoken, yet tenacious and meticulous, he was dubbed "the quiet pioneer" by his son, Peter Leslie, in a book by the same name. Because of his uncanny skill at getting the most ground miles per pound of fuel, Leslie was called "the father of long-range cruising."

As chief Pacific engineer, he was responsible for preparing the S-42 for its transpacific survey flights and the development of the world-renowned M-130 *China Clipper*. He was instrumental in pioneering transatlantic scheduled air service and establishing new routes to many overseas locations, some requiring months at a time away from home in less-than-luxurious conditions.

Though cited for numerous contributions to Pan Am and the industry, Leslie was best known for brilliantly orchestrating one of history's most important flights. After months of top secret planning between the British and US governments, President Franklin Roosevelt, his staff, and Leslie departed for Casablanca, Morocco, on the first unofficial Air Force One, Pan Am's *Dixie Clipper*.

The Casablanca Conference, a meeting between Roosevelt and British Prime Minister Winston Churchill, took place from January 14 to 24, 1943, where they planned the Allied European strategy for the next phase of WWII—the unconditional surrender of the Axis enemies.

As with the present-day Air Force One, not one, but two aircraft, as well as double crews, were involved in the complicated Casablanca mission. In 1943, no sitting president had ever flown on a commercial aircraft—least of all a president with special needs. The public knew that polio-stricken Roosevelt required a wheelchair to move about, but no one, including Leslie, was aware of how severely handicapped he was. Taken by surprise when Roosevelt showed up to board the *Dixie Clipper* in Miami on January 11, Leslie took immediate action to have special ramps built, installed, and finally loaded onto the aircraft for future use at all the en route landing sites. Onboard facilities required last-minute adjustments, and the flight crews had to consider

Juan Trippe and John Leslie. *Courtesy of PAHF.*

additional safety procedures in the event of emergencies. Already dealing with the stress of safely transporting a US president, Leslie and the crew took on the added responsibility of a passenger with a physical handicap. Due to their grace and professionalism, Roosevelt and his staff were barely aware of the extra measures.

During *Dixie Clipper*'s return flight to Miami, Leslie and the crew honored the president with a birthday celebration. The cake's top read "Happy Birthday Chief." Back in Washington, President Roosevelt wrote a personal letter: "Dear Commander Leslie, I want to tell you what a wonderful trip I had and how much I enjoyed it. The arrangements were perfect and I did not have an uncomfortable moment (Leslie 2012)."

Leslie was elected to the Pan Am board of directors in 1950, but shortly after his promotion, Pan Am's hero of the Casablanca trip was stricken with a virulent case of polio that left him in worse condition than Roosevelt. Paralyzed almost entirely from the neck down, for months he hovered near death in an iron lung.

Thereafter, Leslie remained unable to perform simple personal tasks, but true to his problem-solving grit and drive, he designed a device specific for his needs. In admiration, Pan Am mechanics quickly manufactured it, allowing him to return to work.

Leslie remained quadriplegic until the end of his life, regarding his physical limitations with dignity and class—nothing less than expected from Pan Am's "quiet pioneer."

Edwin Charles Musick was hired by Priester to fly Tri-motors and other early aircraft for Philadelphia Rapid Transit Airlines in 1926. A year later, when Trippe brought Priester to Pan Am, the young aviator followed. At the age of only thirty-three, Musick was a WWI veteran and an experienced aviator. Hired as Pan Am's first pilot, he launched a fabled career with the new airline.

Indispensable to Trippe in all matters of flight operations, Musick pioneered routes and aircraft for the next eleven years in South America, the Caribbean, and the Pacific. He was hailed in the annals of aviation history for commanding *China Clipper*'s dramatic first airmail flight from San Francisco to Manila in 1935. His earlier contributions to Pan Am included many other notable firsts.

In 1928, he flew survey and/or mail flights on the S-38 from Key West to Havana, and in the same year from Havana to the Dominican Republic. In 1929, with Trippe and Lindbergh, he was at the controls of Airmail Route #6 to Dutch Guiana. He flew test flights on the S-40s and S-42s in the Caribbean, and from San Francisco to Honolulu, for which he was awarded the coveted Harmon Trophy. In 1935, he was featured on the cover of *Time* magazine.

Like Trippe and Lindbergh, Musick was a shy, private man of few words. He avoided publicity wherever and whenever possible. During his crossing of the Pacific on *China Clipper*, he was asked to describe the Pacific sunset to a riveted radio audience. He responded, "Sunset, 0639 hours (Leslie 2012)."

Captain Musick at Alameda Airport, 1935. Courtesy of PAHF.

Musick's persistence to check and double-check every aspect of a flight earned him a reputation for safety and the nickname "Meticulous Musick." He never hesitated to turn back or abort if he was in doubt about the safety of a flight.

But on January 11, 1938, two hours after departing from American Samoa en route to New Zealand, the *Samoan Clipper* sprang an oil leak. Musick turned back to Pago Pago Harbor, but the plane was too heavy to land. He had two choices: risk flying for several hours until enough fuel had burned off, or dump fuel—a dangerous procedure due to the S-42's design.

The ever-cautious Musick began dumping fuel. The exact cause will never be known, but approaching Samoa, the Clipper exploded in a huge burst of flames that was visible for many miles. The bodies of the seven crewmembers were never recovered.

At the time of his death, Musick had flown more than two million miles. Compared to the most revered pilots of the 1930s, Musick is second only to Charles Lindbergh.

Harold E. Gray joined Pan American Systems as the budding airline's tenth flying boat pilot in 1929. A handsome young man with an impressive list of aviation credentials, in 1934 he was the first captain to be distinguished as Pan Am's Master of the Ocean Flying Boats. During his flying years with Pan Am, Gray flew virtually all the company's flying boats in Central and South America, as well as the critical Atlantic and Pacific crossings.

Captain Harold Gray, 1936. *Courtesy of PAHF.*

Between 1937 and 1939 Gray flew S-42 survey flights to Bermuda, Ireland, Southampton, the Azores, Lisbon, and Marseille, and in 1936, he co-piloted Pan Am's first Pacific passenger flight on the M-130, *Hawaii Clipper*. On March 29–30, 1939, Captain Gray made history on the Boeing 314 *Yankee Clipper* during the first and most demanding transatlantic 2,400-mile flight. Later, in 1941, he piloted the *Cape Town Clipper* on what was then the world's longest round-trip proving route between New York's La Guardia Airport and Léopoldville, Belgian Congo.

By 1944, when Gray was appointed Pan Am's Atlantic Division Operations Manager, he and Juan Trippe had developed a lasting friendship of mutual respect and admiration. In 1952, the board of directors named Gray executive vice president of the Atlantic Division, and in 1959 he was elected to the board. Finally, in July 1964, the board elected Gray president of Pan Am to succeed Trippe when he retired.

Trippe remained as chairman and CEO with high hopes for Gray's successful leadership, but tragically, less than two years after Gray took over as president of Pan American, he was forced to retire due to failing health. Gray, from Guttenberg, Iowa, died on December 23, 1972 at age sixty-six, leaving in his wake a consummate aviation and administrative legacy.

"You Missed the Tea Party!"

(Adapted from *An American Saga* by Robert Daley and *Huffington Post* blog by Dr. Helen Davey)

The year was 1929. Two newly married couples were on a three-week, 9,000-mile adventure. The purpose of their flight was threefold: a combination survey and publicity trip for Pan Am, and the first delivery of US mail to the company's most recently acquired South American destinations.

Charles Lindbergh was at the controls of the noisy twin-engine Sikorsky S-38 as he and Anne and close friends Juan and Betty Trippe prepared to set down at the airport in Barranquilla, Colombia. Anticipating the welcoming celebration, the men wore smart traveling suits. The ladies were decked out in stylish dresses and hats.

Global superstar of the day "Lucky Lindy" circled in vain for forty-five minutes, waiting for the exuberant crowd below to clear the runway. Finally, unsure how much gas was left in the land/amphibian plane, he was forced to go in search of an alternative landing site. Gaining altitude, he headed for a small lagoon spotted earlier deep in the Columbian jungle. At the top of the climb, likely for lack of fuel, both engines suddenly died. In the shocked silence, only Lindbergh spoke. Turning to his speechless passengers, he grinned. "I think we'll make it, but hang on tight!"

Moments later, the lagoon came into sight just in time for the plane to glide onto the marshy surface. As they rocked gently on the lagoon, time ticked by. The surrounding jungle closed in, growing darker and more threatening. Lindbergh was armed with a revolver and snakebite kit, but facing too many unknowns, no one wanted to venture off the aircraft. They decided to simply wait.

At last, in the dim light of dusk, two dugout canoes came toward them. One was full of naked children. In the other were two men wearing nothing but G-strings who signaled for the stranded couples to board the canoes.

The foursome were preparing to climb aboard when Trippe's well-known sense of decorum prevailed over the potentially life-threatening situation. Glancing first at the near-naked men, then at Anne and Betty, he whispered urgently to Lindbergh, "But these men have nothing on! What about the girls?"

It must have been Lindbergh's innate sense of survival that overruled his friend's sensibilities. The fashion plate couples precariously boarded the canoes, and once safely ashore, found a muddy road where they were picked up by a passing car.

Aviatrix and author Ann Lindbergh and author Betty Trippe. *Courtesy of PAHF.*

Meanwhile, at the Barranquilla airport, Lindbergh worshipers continued waiting with rapt enthusiasm under a banner, "Welcome Lindy!" Unaware of the emergency landing and subsequent rescue by scantily clad Columbian natives, one member of the Barranquilla celebration chided Betty and Anne, "You missed the tea party!"

The SS *North Haven* sailed the seven seas for decades, participated in many adventures, and survived two wars. But perhaps her most remarkable feat was transporting the men and materials for Pan American Airways's Pacific flying boat bases. The *North Haven* enabled Pan Am to provide the first transoceanic mail and passenger air service across the world's greatest ocean.

Built in 1919, the *North Haven* was an unremarkable ship by the standards of the early twentieth century. Displacing 4,660 tons and measuring 350 feet from stem to stern, she was of the type seamen dubbed a three-island steamer. The name stems from the silhouette she presented on the horizon; the forecastle, the bridge, and the poop deck showed before the decking—hence the name. Others called her a tramp steamer; although not strictly true, it added to her mystique.

Juan Trippe's dream of flying the Pacific hinged on flying boat bases that could refuel and refit his Clippers. A team of talented professionals, including chief engineer André Priester and junior

SS *North Haven* schematic. Drawing by Jamie Dodson.

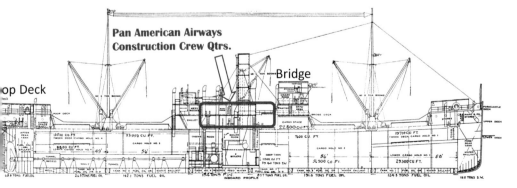

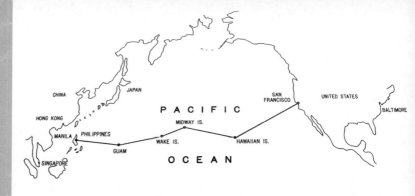

Pan Am's 1935
Pacific Route.
Drawing by
Jamie Dodson.

engineer John G. Borger, developed a detailed plan that included bases on Hawaii, Midway, Wake, Guam, and the Philippines.

At Oahu, Hawaii, and the Philippines, Pan Am could make use of existing facilities and regular freight shipments. The navy offered an abandoned US Marine Corps base on Guam. All that remained was to build two complete bases on the Wake and Midway atolls. Midway had a small transpacific cable operation on Sand Island, but earlier expeditions reported that Wake consisted of a desert group of three atolls, only a few feet above sea level and waterless. Although claimed by the United States, no one was able to determine who administered the archipelago. Despite these and many other uncertainties, Trippe insisted on going ahead.

Captain L. L. Odell, Pan Am's chief airport engineer, was in charge of planning, and Charles Russell was in charge of the expedition. In just two months, eight employees at the Pan American headquarters Chrysler Building, New York, planned the whole expedition. John Borger, later Pan Am vice president of engineering, recalled the enormity of the project: "I was just out of college, and was chief clerk. I remember our Request for Capital Appropriation was over a million dollars, one of the biggest RCAs at the time, but the Board okayed it immediately."

Odell began organizing the expedition on January 7, 1935, and by January 15, production orders started flowing to the manufacturers. Odell sent a revised assignment to Bill Grooch, who was about to sail to China as operations manager of the Far East Division. Instead, Grooch proceeded to San Francisco Pier 22 to take charge of preparing and loading the cargo. He would supervise the storage of tons of material until the cargo could be loaded aboard the ship.

Grooch wrote a detailed memoir about his participation in the first *North Haven* voyage, *Skyway to Asia*, published in 1936. In it he describes hiring a local man named Dan Vucetich, with whom he surveyed the loading area. "We looked over the pier together and made plans for stacking the materials as it arrived. The pier was eight hundred feet long and could accommodate several ships at once. Dan and I thought half the space would be suitable for our needs."

They marked out areas on the warehouse floor based on where the cargo was bound and what was needed first at each location, but when Allen Mittag arrived from New York with the initial material list, they had to revise their plans. Grooch reviewed the list and handed it to Vucetich. He took one look and said, "Boss, we're gonna need a bigger space." The list called for 6,000 tons for the first voyage alone. Odell arrived in mid-March to assist with the final details only a few days before they were to start loading.

The SS *North Haven* docked at Pier 22 on March 23, 1935. On the Pan Am Historical Foundation website, Borger recalled, "The North Haven was the perfect ship for the job. The 6,700-ton [4,660 tons, actually] freighter had been taking cannery workers to Alaska, and its lower deck was a dormitory with double bunks, and we had 112, plus the ship's crew of thirty-two men aboard. It had huge refrigerators, and we had to carry six months' worth of food for Midway and Wake. We had to plan to load it so the things we'd need to unload first were loaded last."

Finally, they began loading the gear. Along with the food, they carried a quarter of a million gallons of aviation gas in fifty-five-gallon drums, forty long-direction finder (DF) antenna masts, two ten-ton tractors, four windmill pumps, four five-ton diesel generators, thousands of gallons of diesel fuel, and prefabricated buildings to construct two small villages on the atolls. They also brought along seeds for gardens, as it might be months before resupplies got back to either atoll with fresh fruits and vegetables.

Personal comfort items for the crew included forty-five books for a lending library, twenty packs of playing cards, pens, pencils and paper, sheets, pillowcases, chewing tobacco, chewing gum, pots and pans, and even two kitchen sinks. It seems that Odell's team thought of everything. Everything, that is, but alcohol. Under no circumstances could any member of the expedition possess alcohol.

Pan Am pulled forty-five men from the Eastern Division and assigned them to the new Pacific Division headed by US Army Col. (retired) Clarence M. Young, a WWI flying ace and former assistant secretary of commerce for aeronautics (1929–33) under President Hoover. Grooch was put in charge of hiring the construction crew. The country was in the grips of the worst economic depression in history, and hundreds of out-of-work tradesman showed up every day in the hopes of landing a job.

Grooch recalled, "I had already picked out a number of men for the construction crew. The news got around, and more and more applicants besieged Pier 22. Some of these men had good jobs, but the expedition promised excitement and adventure, and they were sure to save money since they couldn't spend a cent where we were going."

Leaving HNL aboard the North Haven, March 1935: From left, fron t row: Bill Young; Mr. Ward, commisary; Dr. Kessler; Charles Russell, construction; Bill Gooch, expedition; Frank McKenzie, Wake Airport Engineer. Back row: John Steele, engineer; Mr. Gregory, Guam station manager; John Borger and Bill Taylor, engineers; Karl Lueder, Midway station mgr.

The expedition doctor, Myron L. Kenler, MD, gave each applicant a physical. If the prospect passed, the new guy got a series of vaccinations against tropical diseases. The only man to fail the physical and still sail with the *North Haven* was Bill Young, Col. Young's brother. Over Kenler's strong objections and those of Grooch, Col. Young approved his brother's participation. It was a decision the colonel would regret for the rest of his long life.

On March 27, 1935, the *North Haven* set sail, her decks crowded with four oceangoing launches, three lighters, and the holds full of $500,000 worth of cargo ($8.7 million in today's dollars). Unlike the Matson Ocean Liners that plied the Hawaii trade, the *North Haven* was not built for speed. She was built to haul cargo economically and could make only ten knots.

The weather those first few days was miserable, especially for landlubbers on their initial ocean voyage. A nasty swell from the northwest ploughed into the ship's starboard beam, causing an alarming roll. The launches and lighters strapped to the deck raised the ship's center of gravity, worsening the degree and duration of the roll. The ship's company and those with nautical experience, like Grooch, were unaffected, but eighty or so men took to their bunks with a distinct green cast to their complexions. Below deck took on a smell that managed to overpower the stench of fish from the ship's former life. Some men became so dehydrated that Dr. Kenler had to order them to sick bay and administer intravenous fluids.

When all but the sickest gained their sea legs, Grooch set up seamanship classes on the many nautical subjects they would need to learn. Several of the men chosen to operate the launches also needed to learn celestial navigation. Eventually, Grooch turned the new navigators loose to shoot the sun and the stars and calculate their positions. The initial results were interesting: some gave their position as a little north of the South Pole; others were sure they were sailing on Lake Michigan; and the most adamant was convinced they were seven miles west of Moscow.

Finally, on Thursday, April 4, 1935, the *North Haven* arrived at Honolulu Harbor. Perhaps it was the prospect of more days at sea on the wallowing *North Haven*, or perhaps it was seeing the Hawaiian paradise for the first time, but several members of the construction crew jumped ship and were never heard from again. This placed Grooch in a tough position. He needed to replace the men he'd lost, but he had to do it while loading a "special cargo."

Word got out quickly that the expedition needed men, and soon the dock was crowded with fortune-seekers and scalawags. Disgusted, Grooch gave the hiring job to Vucetich and turned his attention to that "special cargo"—tons of TNT. When all was ready, the Honolulu harbormaster came aboard and asked for a cargo manifest. When he realized that the *North Haven* held hundreds of drums of highly volatile liquids and was loading tons of TNT, he asked that they be extremely careful. As he put it, "Should there be an explosion, most of the harbor and indeed Honolulu would go up in cinders."

Grooch asked, "Where will you be should there be trouble?"

The harbormaster replied, "On the other side of the island."

With the aid of some of the construction crew, Grooch was able to stow the TNT without incident. Meanwhile, Vucetich hired suitable replacements. When they shuffled aboard, an athletic young man named William J. Mullahey came along. He was wearing a Hawaiian shirt, shorts, a straw hat, and was carrying an army surplus haversack on his back. He had a ukulele tucked under one arm and a surfboard under the other. When Vucetich asked who he was, Mullahey replied, "Mr. Odell hired me by phone from San Francisco. Said he needed an underwater explosive expert." After a few days at sea, Mullahey told Kenler, "I'm not exactly sure what an underwater explosive expert might be, but I'm game."

An earlier US Navy survey had determined that the Wake lagoon was festooned with coral heads, which, in order to create a safe landing site for flying boats, would have to be blasted out with dynamite. Oblivious to the danger of his undertaking, the carefree Mullahey would not only survive, but would become a living Pan Am legend. In 1941, after taking over the station manager position at Auckland, New Zealand, he again played an essential role only hours after the bombing of Pearl Harbor by dispatching the *Pacific Clipper* on its history-making trip around the globe.

Knot class aboard SS *North Haven*. Courtesy of PAHF.

The *North Haven* left Honolulu with great fanfare and set a course for Midway. She pitched and wallowed another four days to reach the atoll, which consists of two small islands surrounded by a ring of coral reefs. Grooch described it as "a dirty smudge on the horizon." The long Pacific rollers continually crashed against the reefs, creating huge breakers, columns of spray, and thunderous roars.

The ship hove to off the south shore of Sand Island, the larger of Midway's two coral atolls, and dropped anchor. They were soon approached by a fast-moving motor launch, punching its way through the heavy surf. When the launch tied up alongside, two men, drenched from crossing the reef, climbed the gangway. Grooch met them at the rail. They introduced themselves as Mr. Perry, the cable station manager, and Mr. Lawn, the chief engineer. They informed Grooch that only the western approach to the lagoon could be used. It was far more exposed to ocean swells and much more dangerous, but the southern approach held the Pacific cable—off limits to deep keel launches.

In an open ocean, the arduous task of swinging the cargo over the side onto the lighters began. Below, the lighters bobbed dangerously up and down in the swell at a far greater rate than the 10,000-ton ship. The *North Haven*'s derrick operators had to gauge the transfer with perfect timing to avoid putting a load through the bottom of a lighter or on top of a stevedore.

Crossing the western reef was another challenge. The launch skipper, or coxswain, would tow one or sometimes two lighters from the *North Haven* to "The Hook," the ominous name for the westernmost part of the reef. There, he would wait until a large roller made its way toward them. At just the right moment, he would jam the twin diesel throttles forward and catch the wave at its crest. Then, with skillful manipulation, the coxswain would try to keep the launch on top of the wave. It was a difficult maneuver but the only way to get sufficient water depth to clear the rudder and prop. The lighters drew much less water and would normally clear the reef without incident, though, on several occasions, the men riding the lighters reported slamming into the reef. One man was tossed overboard, but was able to reach the lighter safely.

When they got to shore, the men loaded the cargo on four-by-twenty-foot sleds that Borger had designed, then the tractors towed them into place. Despite the dangers, there was only one major injury among several minor incidents. Careful planning and wide

safety margins saved many a limb, even a life or two. Despite the unexpected hardships, they were only four days behind the schedule Odell had worked out in New York. The men's arduous work and perseverance made all the difference.

Once the crew unloaded Midway's cargo, the *North Haven* sailed for Wake with forty-six construction workers. The rest remained with Pan Am technicians to finish the Midway base. Fewer men on board immensely eased the earlier below-decks crowding, and for the first time since leaving San Francisco, the crew enjoyed a more relaxed schedule—relaxed for everyone except Dr. Kenler and Bill Young.

During the strenuous work at Midway, Young had started coughing blood. Kenler placed him in sickbay, but his condition worsened. Concerned about Young's deteriorating condition, Kenler went to Grooch with his fears. Grooch burned up the airwaves until he reached the USS *Henderson*, which was transiting from Honolulu to Guam. Although well past the *North Haven's* position, the *Henderson* turned back and sailed at top speed to meet up with the *North Haven* at sea. As Young's crewmates cheered a hearty farewell, the *Henderson's* captain took him aboard and made all possible speed to reach the Naval Hospital on Guam.

As the *Henderson* steamed away, Grooch turned to Kenler, "Doc, what do you think his chances are?"

Kenler shook his head. "Not good, Bill. He should never have come along."

Collectively, Wake consists of three coral atolls—Peale, Wilkes, and Wake itself. All were uninhabited until Pan Am built the flying

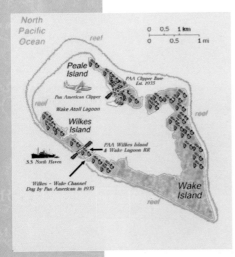

Wake Atoll.
*Drawing by
Jamie Dodson.*

boat base. Initially Pan Am planned to locate the flying boat station on Wilkes Island, which is open to the sea, but the survey team found it was too low in the water and would flood during storms. Instead, George Bicknell, Wake's airport manager, along with Grooch, selected Peale Island. However, Peale was on the far side of the lagoon, inaccessible from the ocean side. This meant the men would have to unload the cargo at a storage yard on Wilkes and then drag it across the island to the lagoon. According to Grooch, Captain Odell had ordered the steel rails as support poles for an extra radio tower. However, once on Wake, Borger and others fashioned them into railroad tracks. Borger later commented, "Someone had the brilliant idea of building a fifty-yard railroad to the lagoon."

Just when everything seemed to be running smoothly, a new problem arose. There was no easy way to get the small launch into

Wilkes Island
Rail Road.
*Courtesy of
PAHF.*

the lagoon. Grooch decided to put it on a barge; then, aided by the tractor, the Wake crew shoved it across the knee-deep channel between Wake and Wilkes. The indispensable launch towed barges across the lagoon to Peale, where the tractor pulled sleds of cargo into position.

Moving the
Wake launch
through the
shallows into
the Lagoon.
*Courtesy of
PAHF.*

Next Borger and Bill Mullahey had to clear the coral heads to provide a six-foot-deep open area for the Clipper landings. Once again the railroad track came in handy. Borger and Mullahey hung a length of it to a depth of six feet from under a barge while a launch towed them back and forth across the lagoon. It was boring work and hot as blazes, so the two men often nodded off. But when the track hit coral, it made a loud clang, shaking the barge. Startled awake, Mullahey and Borger threw off cork buoys attached to anchors. Later, Borger rowed a small boat back to the marked spot, and Mullahey donned bamboo goggles of his own design. While diving to inspect the coral heads, he also armed himself with a bamboo spear in case he spotted any fish for dinner.

"The snorkel had yet to be invented, so Mullahey held his breath," Borger recalled. "When he surfaced, he would ask for six, or eight, sticks of dynamite, then he dove back down and tied them to the coral. When Mullahey resurfaced, I rowed upwind as far as possible. Once at a safe distance, Mullahey pressed a magneto button and blew up the coral."

After the explosion, they rowed back to recover any fish killed by the blast. Along with Mullahey's speared catch, fresh fish made them very popular with the other men, who had grown sick of the canned food provisions.

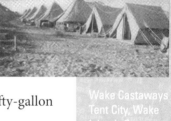

The dynamite duo continued until they had cleared a pie-shaped landing area with the point located near the Peale dock. They marked the entire area with empty fifty-gallon diesel drums.

While the construction crew continued to labor on Wake, Grooch made plans to take the *North Haven* to Guam and Manila, where he needed to deliver radio equipment and pick up more aviation gas. Confident that Grooch would be able to find a replacement launch on Guam, Bicknell talked him into leaving the Wake launch behind, a decision Grooch would later regret.

The night before departure, all hands were present at the newly completed Peale Island mess hall where the *North Haven's* farewell dinner turned into a rowdy affair. Despite the alcohol prohibition, no one was surprised to see eight brown jugs of local-made "jungle juice" sitting in the place of honor at the head table. One by one, the men came up and filled their coffee mugs with the potent brew, and before long, the effects became apparent. In less than perfect harmony, the well-oiled men broke into boisterous songs of Ireland, England, and lost love.

The *North Haven's* master, Captain Borklund, a naturalized Swede of unknown origins, stood up unsteadily at the head table. He swayed and came close to falling, but caught himself before teetering over. Moments later, he began a long, impassioned speech in an unknown language. The guests looked at each other, clueless.

Captain
Borklund,
Master of the
SS *North Haven.*
Courtesy of
PAHF.

They were unsure what Borklund said, but most agreed it was probably Swedish. Nevertheless, when Borklund concluded, every able-bodied man rose on unsteady feet in raucous cheers. Others toppled over backward as the hall dissolved into roars of laughter.

At that moment, Grooch managed to climb onto a table. "Everyone charge your cups!" he slurred in a booming voice. "Gentlemen, lift your drinks! Let me start with the traditional toast a naval officer gives at formal gatherings: To the United States of America—Land of the Free!"

By now, well into the spirit *and* the spirits, the Wake Castaways, as they came to be known, raised their coffee mugs. Grooch continued toasting the navy, the captain, the crew, Pan American, and anyone or anything else that came to mind.

Revelry in the mess hall of that isolated atoll continued long into an endless starlit night. Repeatedly backslapping each other, the men roared with laughter and sang with great gusto. Accompanied only by the background pounding surf, no one else on the planet could hear them.

It was a subdued, hung-over crew that sailed the proverbial morning after. Making stops at Guam and Manila, Grooch's crew delivered the radio equipment and picked up the fuel, as planned, but on the return through Guam, he faced the task of locating a replacement launch for Wake. Cursing himself for listening to Bicknell, who had assured him the navy would supply the needed vessel, he soon discovered they were no help. Running out of time, and in desperation, he purchased a launch from a private party, but by the time Grooch realized what poor shape it was in, the seller refused to take it back. Still cursing Bicknell, he knew he was stuck with it. Frustrated and out of options, he loaded it aboard the *North Haven* and headed back to Wake.

The Wake Castaways became ingenious, resourceful, and innovative on more than a few occasions. Against daunting odds, they devised ways to overcome the geographical limitations of Wake, unload and deliver the supplies and equipment to the best possible locations, and install all the equipment for Wake's operations. In addition, they had to figure out their own survival needs, which the Pan Am planners in New York had overlooked.

Unlike Midway, Wake had no potable ground water. Cleverly, the men rigged canvas catches on the roofs of their tents, which drained rainwater into underground tanks. Windmills pumped the water throughout the camp.

In another moment of inspiration, the Wake Castaways employed the use of leftover thirty-five-foot antenna masts for the end of a

400-foot dock. The improvised antenna masts not only created a highly functional landing float for the Clippers, but cut down on the number of coral heads Mullahey and Borger needed to blast.

Returning from Guam, the *North Haven* dropped anchor off Wake on the morning of July 3, when Grooch delivered sad news. He'd gone to visit Bill Young in the Naval Hospital where he'd learned that Young had succumbed to his consumption (tuberculosis). The navy doctor said he would most probably have died regardless of his participation in the expedition. Years later, Col. Young spoke often about his brother— about his courage to be part of something larger than himself, despite his deteriorating health. He speculated that Bill must have suspected he was dying –probably the reason why he'd argued so vehemently to be included on the *North Haven's* manifest.

After Grooch delivered the flimsy, leaking launch, he became the butt of many a joke. The Guam launch's ancient motor was known to sputter and die without warning, usually at the most inconvenient places, farthest away from the base. Loathed by all, it nevertheless became a humorous part of the Wake Castaways's legend.

A few days after the derelict launch arrived on Wake, Grooch and most of the crew set sail for San Francisco on the *North Haven*. She would return six months later with the second Pan Am shipment. Back on Peale, Borger and Bicknell continued their daily recordings of wind speed, direction, and weather. Both men repeatedly confirmed that the wind consistently blew from the southeast. Viewed from the air, the two runways blasted out of the coral formed an "X" in the lagoon. Short on time, Bicknell decided to lengthen the runway that aligned with the prevailing wind and delay clearing the other perpendicular runway.

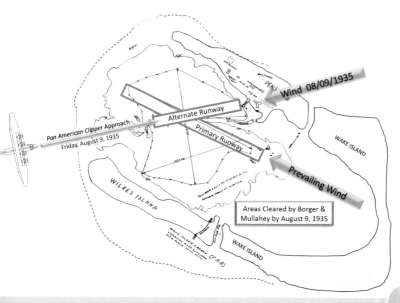

Wake Archipelago landing area sketch. *By Jamie Dodson.*

But, as fate would have it, on August 9, 1935, the wind blew from the northeast. This was the day that captains Robert Oliver Daniel (Rod) Sullivan and Jack Tilton were scheduled to arrive aboard the *Pan American Clipper* on an important survey mission.

The aberrant wind direction meant that the S-42 would have to land on the shorter runway rather than the longer one. Tension was palpable as the Wake Castaways watched the Sikorsky make its final approach. It was possible the huge flying boat would not be able to stop before plowing into the newly improvised floating dock. Seconds ticked by like hours. During the final moments, the *Pan American Clipper* slid onto the water in a perfect landing, coming to a stop just in time to avoid hitting the floating dock. Both experienced captains had more than proven their worth to Pan Am. However, Captain Sullivan, known to be temperamental and outspoken, soon expressed his rage in colorful language.

Sikorsky S-42A, *Pan American Clipper* at Wake Pier. *Courtesy of PAHF.*

Weeks passed as the remaining men on Midway and Wake prepared for the arrival of the new Martin M-130 Ocean Transport, known to the world as the *China Clipper.* Under the driving force of William Van Dusen, Pan Am's media department worked overtime to ensure the historic event was covered worldwide.

On November 22, 1935, the *China Clipper* took off from Alameda Airport, California, embarking on the first transpacific airmail flight. A crowd of more than 25,000 people came out to witness the historic departure of the craft hailed as the "greatest airplane ever built." Stashed in its cargo bay were 115,000 letters weighing almost two tons. As *China Clipper* approached Honolulu the next afternoon, a squadron of sixty US Army and Navy airplanes provided a spectacular escort to Pearl Harbor (for more on *China Clipper*, see chapter 4). Though with far less fanfare on Midway and Wake, the great silver bird's arrival at both atolls was equally important to Pan Am's ongoing monumental aviation achievements.

The M-130 *China Clipper* flying boat was under the command of Chief Pilot Captain Edwin C. Musick. Global coverage was entirely focused on the aircraft, the esteemed captain, and his crew of six. Ignored and overlooked were countless other "down-line" Pan Am employees, with no mention of the *North Haven's* essential role.

In January 1936, the *North Haven* again set sail from San Francisco to Midway and Wake. This time her hold contained two complete prefabricated luxury hotels with all the furnishings. Her cold storage was stuffed with sufficient frozen food to accommodate the guests for months. She also carried skilled craftsmen who would assemble the structures, install the wiring and electric lines from the generators, and fit the plumbing.

After making the delivery, the *North Haven* and her crew sailed back to San Francisco. As usual, Trippe had insisted on what seemed like an impossible schedule, but the hardworking, professional craftsmen at Midway and Wake were able to finish the job on time. As a reward, many returned to Honolulu on the M-130 Clipper mail runs. From there, they took ship's passages back to the Bay Area. Otherwise, the intrepid, heroic, and ingenious crewmembers of the *North Haven* were lost to history.

Almost a year later, as planned, Pan Am's mail route became a passenger route. Trippe's fascination with maritime habits continued, as noted by inaugural passenger Lauren Lyman:

"Clipper is a ship, not a plane. Time is marked by bells, the crew's watches are set at Greenwich Mean Time, and everything on board moves according to the best merchant maritime practice. As with ships, a steward oversaw the passenger cabin, helping with customs and immigration forms, and organizing luggage. He kept smokers stocked with a steady supply of gum to help them cope with the no smoking rule. He served the meals, which were prepared in advance

and stored in insulated containers to keep them hot. Along with lunch and dinner, which consisted of four courses, there were regular snacks and tea. Alcohol, however, had to be imbibed on the ground."

Thanks to two carefully planned voyages of the *North Haven*, and along with her remarkable crew, Pan Am built the essential Pacific bases. But the North Haven's time with Pan Am soon came to an end. Even though shipborne resupplies to the atolls continued for many years, smaller vessels would accomplish the deliveries.

The *North Haven* returned to her previous life, continuing to ply the Pacific for another eighteen years. During WWII, she carried US Marines to their assault beaches and brought them needed supplies. She survived dive-bombers, submarines, and even a Kamikaze attack off Okinawa. She reprised her role during the Korean War and participated in MacArthur's Inchon landing.

In 1950, her Pacific odyssey ended when a Panamanian firm bought her. Re-flagged and renamed the SS *Georgiana*, she began to sail the Caribbean Sea. Tragically, on May 12, 1953, the captain ran her aground off the coast of Puerto Rico. Declared a total loss, she was broken up and sold as scrap within a month.

And so ended the storied life of a remarkable ship—remarkable for her numerous contributions to America's war efforts, as well as her utterly essential role in the commercial conquest of the Pacific Ocean. Together, the *North Haven* and Pan American accomplished one of the greatest feats in aviation history.

he Debut of the China Clipper

CHAPTER 4

S he was one of the great beauties of her day. With her pert,
upturned nose and graceful lines, she drew appreciative looks
wherever she appeared. Her list of admirers included presidents,
generals, movie stars, builders of empires. Her name was *China
Clipper*, and when she made her debut on the afternoon of November
22, 1935, the world watched in wonder.

*China Clipper
send-off at
the airport
in Alameda,
California.
Courtesy of
PAHF.*

It was a perfect day for making history. San Francisco Bay sparkled like a field of jewels. Twenty-five thousand people had crowded onto the Alameda seaplane base. The band played a Sousa march while a young airline founder named Juan Trippe led the speakers to the platform. Behind the reviewing stand waited the star of the show, her silver wings forming the backdrop for the ceremony. The entire event was being broadcast by CBS and NBC and transmitted live on seven foreign networks.

She was the largest airliner yet constructed in America. The *China Clipper*'s streamlined shape was a radical departure from the wire-bound, strut-braced machines of the day. Until she was built, no transport aircraft existed that could carry both a payload and the vast store of fuel required to reach the distant bases of the Pacific.

On the reviewing stand, Postmaster General James Farley conducted a ceremonial loading of mailbags. Then he read a message from President Roosevelt: "Even at this distance, I thrill to the wonder of it all . . ."

At this, a smile crept across Trippe's face. He knew precisely to whom the credit for the wonder should go. In only eight years, from a company with no assets or airplanes or routes, Trippe had built Pan American into America's premier international airline.

When Trippe announced his intention to send the *China Clipper* across the Pacific, a chorus of so-called experts had argued against it. Such an undertaking was too dangerous, they said, at least for a commercial airline. Such stunts should be left to the military. The Pacific was too wide, too filled with unknowns. The craft of aerial navigation was still too primitive, and the new radio direction finders had yet to be proven. The big flying boat, they liked to point out, had never actually flown across an ocean, not even as far as Hawaii.

Trippe knew all this. He went ahead with his plans.

When the postmaster finished speaking, a radio announcer took over. "On the wings of these sturdy clipper ships," he told his audience, "are pinned the hopes of America's commerce for a rightful standing in the teeming markets of the Orient." The script had been written by Trippe's handpicked publicity director, an imaginative

Debut of the China Clipper

The *China Clipper*'s maiden flight from San Francisco Bay in November 1935 was the culmination of Pan Am's meteoric rise in the 1920s and '30s. The landmark event was broadcast live over nine radio networks, reaching millions of people on four continents. One of the era's most listened-to events, it was a forerunner of worldwide coverage given to Apollo 11 more than a quarter-century later when NASA put Neil Armstrong on the moon.

China Clipper was one of the most famous airplanes of all time due to her conquest of the Pacific Ocean, which took years of planning, explosive innovation, and the efforts of hundreds of men and women who hurdled innumerable obstacles.

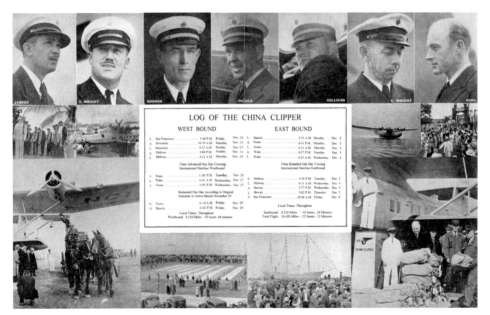

China Clipper inaugural flight log with crew. *Courtesy of PAHF.*

young man named William Van Dusen. For today's inaugural ceremony, Van Dusen had outdone himself.

Dressed in their all-black, double-breasted uniforms and navy-style caps, the seven-man crew marched aboard the *China Clipper*. The captain was a slender, soft-spoken man, forty-one years old, who was known among his fellow airmen as "Meticulous Musick." Ed Musick believed in precision in everything from the knot in his tie to the finest details of an ocean flight. Only eleven days before, Musick and his crew had taken delivery of the new flying boat from the Glenn L. Martin factory in Middle River, Maryland. Now they were about to fly the new ship westward, across the widest part of the world's widest ocean.

Over the loudspeakers crackled radio transmissions from the five ocean bases along the Clipper's route to the Orient—Honolulu, Midway, Wake, Guam, and Manila. Each declared it was ready to commence Pan American's transpacific service.

One after another, the *China Clipper's* four Pratt & Whitney engines rumbled to life. The lines were cast off while the band struck up "The Star-Spangled Banner." As the Clipper glided out into the bay, Trippe's voice boomed over the radio and the loudspeakers, "Captain Musick, you have your sailing orders. Cast off and depart for Manila in accordance therewith." Twenty-two aerial bombs exploded over the bay. Ships' whistles blew, and fire hoses streamed geysers of water.

The thunder of the radial engines echoed from the buildings on the shore. The giant ship surged ahead, aimed westward toward the spans of the unfinished San Francisco-Oakland Bay Bridge. It had been Ed Musick's plan to fly over the bridge, but the heavily loaded Clipper wouldn't climb. At the last instant, with the steel mass of the bridge filling his windscreen, Musick changed the script. He nosed the Clipper back toward the water and zoomed beneath the bridge, between the massive girders and under the hanging cables. Directly on the Clipper's tail came a swarm of escorting airplanes, their pilots all thinking this was part of the show. While thousands of spectators watched from the shores of the bay, the Clipper slowly gained altitude and pointed her nose toward the open Pacific. Gradually her silver silhouette disappeared from view.

By nightfall the *China Clipper* was in smooth air, flying between layers of cloud. In the red-lighted cockpit, Fred Noonan, the Clipper's navigator, labored over his

Martin M-130 *China Clipper* dives under the unfinished Bay Bridge. *Courtesy of PAHF.*

© CLYDE SUNDERLAND OAKLAND

Frederick Joseph Noonan was used to facing peril and uncertainty long before he signed on with Amelia Earhart to navigate her ill-fated, round-the-world flight. He'd held a distinguished two-decade career at sea on merchant ships and served as an ammunitions officer during WWI, surviving the sinking of three ships by German U-boats.

The tall, lanky, blue-eyed man from Cook County, Illinois, navigated Pan Am's first Sikorsky S-42 out of San Francisco in 1935, as well as the *China Clipper's* 1935 maiden voyage. He was also responsible for charting many of Pan Am's Pacific routes to Midway, Wake, Guam, the Philippines, and Hong Kong. As a licensed sea captain, he was known to carry a ship's sextant on all his flights.

During the early 1930s, he worked for Pan Am as a navigation instructor at the company's training school in Miami, later acting as Pan Am's airport manager at Port-au-Prince, Haiti.

By the time Earhart offered him the job of circumnavigating the globe on her twin-engine Lockheed Model 10-E, Noonan had already marked his place in aviation history, but having just divorced and having left Pan American, he was in transition. In search of new horizons, the adventurous Noonan seized the once-in-a-lifetime opportunity.

As history documents, Amelia Earhart and Fred Noonan vanished in flight on July 2, 1937, between Lae, New Guinea, and uninhabited Howland Island. They were both declared dead two years later after exhaustive searches found no traces of them or the airplane.

Pan Am navigator Frederick Joseph Noonan. *Courtesy of PAHF.*

chart table, plotting radio direction finder bearings. When he spotted a break in the cloud cover, Noonan donned his fur-lined flying suit and leather helmet and went to the aft cabin where he opened the hatch atop the Clipper's fuselage. Standing in the roaring wind stream, Noonan took celestial shots with his navigator's octant. Like most early aerial navigators, Noonan didn't trust fixes taken through the glass of an airplane's hatch, worrying that the glass refracted the incoming light of the star.

Each crewmember alternated two hours on duty with a break in the rest bunk. Musick and First Officer "Rod" Sullivan swapped command in the cockpit, and George King, the junior flight officer, took over Noonan's job while the navigator catnapped in the bunk. The flight engineers, C. D. Wright and Vic Wright (the two were unrelated), rotated duty at the engineer's station.

Every half hour William Jarboe, the *China Clipper's* radio operator, transmitted position reports back to Alameda where Van Dusen was tracking the Clipper's progress on a huge map of the Pacific in the lobby of the seaplane base. With each update from the *China Clipper*, the tireless Van Dusen would crank out a fresh press release.

Dawn overtook the Clipper as slowly as the night had fallen eight hours before. Peering into the murky gray horizon, the pilots looked for the first signs of landfall. When they were still 200 miles from Honolulu, Sullivan let out a shout. He spotted the massive cone of Mauna Kea on the Big Island jutting from the cloud deck. Another hour passed, then another shout. On the horizon appeared the dark silhouette of Diamond Head. The island of Oahu was in sight.

At 10:10 a.m.—twenty hours and thirty-three minutes after her departure from Alameda—the *China Clipper's* sleek hull touched down on the surface of Pearl Harbor. The longest leg of the 2,395-mile transpacific journey was behind her.

A welcoming ceremony of hula dancers and an abundance of flower lei awaited the *China Clipper* and her crew in Honolulu. Later, while the airmen rested overnight, the Clipper was loaded with staples for the new island bases in the Pacific—cartons of fresh vegetables, turkeys for the staffs' first Thanksgiving on the atolls, crates containing paint, typewriter ribbons, baseballs, tennis racquets, hardware for a complete barber shop.

The flight to Midway, only 1,380 miles, would be the easiest segment of the transpacific voyage. Flying in smooth, ripple-free air, the airmen needed only the strand of islands—Kaua'i, Ni'ihau, Nihoa, Necker, French Frigate Shoals, Gardner Pinnacles, Laysan Island—all pointing like signposts to the US-operated station of Midway Atoll.

The *China Clipper* swept in low over the base at Midway, touching down at 2:01 in the afternoon—one minute off schedule. As the Clipper taxied to the mooring float, the crew could see the white-coated Pan Am staff waiting for them. Buildings were freshly painted, the grounds landscaped, flags flying at their masts. The former cable station outpost had been transformed into a Pan American transpacific ocean base.

At dawn the next morning, the Clipper was airborne. The 1,260-mile leg from Midway to Wake, a tiny two-and-a-half-square-mile sand spit barely awash in the ocean, was the most challenging navigational feat on the transpacific route. Unlike the easy flight to Midway, there were no signposts leading to Wake, no chain of atolls pointing the way, only a thousand miles of trackless ocean. There were no alternate landing sites for Wake and not enough fuel for a return trip to Midway.

Fred Noonan was one of the world's most experienced aerial navigators. For this daylight flight, Noonan's only navigational aids were the sun, an occasional night glimpse of Venus, his own dead reckoning skills, and the new Adcock Direction Finder (invented and patented by British engineer Frank Adcock in 1919), a capricious device that no one, including Noonan, yet trusted.

One of the navigational techniques pioneered by Noonan was called "aim off," a way to ensure that a vessel didn't overshoot a tiny target like Wake Atoll. The navigator would deliberately direct a course to one side of his destination. When he had intercepted a north-south line of position computed on the sun's angle, he would turn and fly along the sun line to the target. Aim off was not precise, but it solved the problem of knowing on which side—north or south—the *China Clipper* was from Wake. Noonan's calculations on that day were precise. Two minutes before the crew spotted the tiny island, the Pan Am staff on Wake radioed that they had the inbound flying boat in sight. Five minutes ahead of schedule, the Clipper settled onto the newly lengthened and deepened marine runway in Wake's lagoon.

Another dawn. Another takeoff from a reef-encircled atoll. The *China Clipper* thundered across Wake's lagoon, breaking free of the water and pointing her bow toward Guam, 1,560 miles to the west. As the sun rose in the sky behind them, the crew opened the Clipper's windows, flooding the cabin with a river of warm tropical air. Musick experimented with different altitudes, hunting for tailwinds that would speed them along the route. He found them at 8,000 feet, covering the final 160 miles to Guam in less than an hour.

And then a glitch. After their triumphant arrival in Guam's Apra Harbor, Musick discovered that all their precise flight planning had been in vain. Though the Clipper had landed exactly on schedule in Guam, he learned that the arrival celebration in Manila was planned for two days hence. Someone in public relations had been confused about the International Date Line. It was too late and too embarrassing to reschedule the ceremony. Ed Musick and his crew, grumbling, were forced to spend an unwanted day off in Guam.

On the morning of Friday, November 29, *China Clipper* lifted from the surface of Apra Harbor and set off for the Philippines. The Guam-to-Manila segment was the last leg of the voyage, and the only one that hadn't been flown during the transpacific feasibility testing. Musick wasn't worried. By now the *China Clipper* had proven herself to be a reliable and sturdy vessel. Musick and his crew prepared themselves for a grand arrival in Manila.

It was grander than they could have imagined. The ceremonies in Alameda and Honolulu had been spectacular, but the reception awaiting the *China Clipper* in Manila surpassed them all. Musick flew a victory lap around the city, then turned the Clipper into the wind and alighted on the slick water of Manila Bay. Directly behind the Clipper roared a swarm of fighter planes, zooming overhead in salute. A hundred small launches escorted the flying boat as she taxied to her landing barge. A hundred thousand excited greeters lined the shore, all waving and cheering the *China Clipper* and her crew.

Through flower-covered arches, the smiling crew walked ashore. Newsreel cameras whirred as Musick presented a letter from President Roosevelt to Philippine President Manuel L. Quezon. There was a parade, a banquet, an official reception. Reporters hounded Musick wherever he went in Manila, hoping for colorful comments. Musick,

China Clipper arrives in Manila, Philippines. Courtesy of PAHF.

perhaps the most laconic of all aviation pioneers, stayed true to form: "Without incident," he said, explaining in two words one of the most significant achievements in aviation history.

Despite Musick's aversion to publicity, he couldn't escape becoming a celebrity. The historic flight of the *China Clipper* earned him the prestigious Harmon Trophy, until then, won by only two other Americans, Charles Lindbergh and Wiley Post. The cover of *Time* magazine featured Musick's face. The publicity-shy aviator was besieged with requests for interviews. Whether he liked it or not, Capt. Ed Musick had become an authentic American hero.

Musick wasn't the only celebrity. A *China Clipper* craze swept Depression-weary America. The very name—*China Clipper*—conjured a spell of adventure. California to Asia in six days! The sense of wonder was the same Americans would feel a generation later during the Apollo missions.

A popular song took her name, then a dance step to the same music. A 1936 Warner Brothers movie, *China Clipper*, starred Humphrey Bogart as Musick and Pat O'Brien as a tough, single-minded airline boss, clearly modeled on Juan Trippe. Within a year all three Martin M-130s had entered service. The *China Clipper* was joined on the transpacific routes by her sister ships, the *Philippine Clipper* and the *Hawaii Clipper*.

On October 21, 1936, after nearly a year of scheduled mail flights, the *China Clipper* inaugurated Pan American's transpacific passenger service. Juan Trippe's bold dream of a Pacific air route had become a reality.

The *China Clipper's* moment on the world's stage lasted only a few years. She was eclipsed by larger and faster flying boats. Then all were swept up in the tumult of WWII. When the war ended, so had the romantic era of the great flying boats. Mighty ships like the *China Clipper* and her sisters passed into history.

The magic of her name remains, still etched in history on that sparkling day in 1935, when a great beauty named *China Clipper* astonished the world and changed forever the concept of international travel.

China Clipper DVD, a 1936 Warner Brothers release. Photo Courtesy of Jamie Dodson.

Nuts & Bolts

Thomas Kewin

CHAPTER 5

We called NC 14716 our "Sweet Sixteen," partly because her registration number ended in the number sixteen, but also because she was the only Martin M-130 left of the original three delivered to Pan Am in 1935. The *Hawaii Clipper* disappeared in a violent storm between Guam and Manila in 1938, followed by the *Philippine Clipper's* crash in the mountains of Santa Rosa, California, in January 1943. Pan Am employees felt a special affection for our "Sweet Sixteen" as the last of the breed and with a legendary history. She was otherwise known as the *China Clipper*.

Like most twenty-year-olds, I thought I was armor-plated, completely invincible. The risks and dangers of a flying career never occurred to me, and in March 1943, I was hired by Pan American Airways Systems as a flight engineer. After five months of training on Treasure Island in San Francisco, I was assigned my first trip on board the fabled *China Clipper* to Hawaii.

Strong west winds and turbulence made the twenty-two hours a butt-numbing flight. The engineer's station was located in the pylon area under the wing, with the seat mounted on vertical struts supporting the rear wing spar. Through small windows on each side, I could see the bottoms of the engines and could hear them loud and clear. I could feel every vibration. The noise was so loud our communication headsets were practically useless. To compensate, we had a telegraph of sorts, connected by cables to signal what the pilots wanted: Start engines, takeoff power, etc. But it wasn't properly rigged, so the captain just waggled the lever to get my attention and then gave me hand signals. The pilots were about fifteen feet ahead of me down a ramp, and I wondered how the hell I would get out of my station in the event of a crash.

After reaching my room at the Moana Hotel, I put on my swimming trunks and threaded through the wartime rolls of barbed wire on Waikiki Beach. I tried some bodysurfing and grabbed a hamburger at the Outrigger Canoe Club (located at that time between the Moana and Royal Hawaiian hotels), then returned to my room. I hadn't slept for thirty-six hours, so, after a long soak in the tub, I hit the bed, going down like a wet chain, and slept for twelve hours.

For the next two nights at the Moana, I could still hear the roar of the engines and feel the vibrations. Maybe I wasn't armor-plated after all. I decided that flying wasn't for me, and planned to resign when I got back to San Francisco, where I hoped to get a job as a ground mechanic. But the return trip was on a beautiful Boeing 314.

Unlike the noisy, vibrating engineer's cubbyhole on the Martin, I found my station positioned with the rest of the crew on the spacious twenty-one-by-nine-foot flight deck. The pilots could close blackout curtains behind their seats to improve their night vision and, at the same time, allow normal lighting in the rest of the flight deck. The exhaust pipes on the B-314 were located on top of the engines, so the sound was carried over the wing, sparing the flight deck and passenger cabins from the roaring noise. The Boeing was an entirely different flying experience.

When Juan Trippe ordered the Martin M-130s in 1934, he had planned to use them for flights from New York to London with possible stops at Gander or Botwood, Newfoundland, and Foynes, Ireland. In those days, the mother's milk of the airline industry was carrying mail cargo at $2 per mile. Passengers and other cargo were only secondary benefits.

By 1935, it was apparent the British wouldn't permit Pan Am access to the ports they controlled until they could produce an aircraft that could cross the Atlantic for their flag carrier, Imperial Airlines (later B.O.A.C. and British Airways). Just as Pan Am needed long-haul aircraft to cross the Pacific, the British needed them to cross the Atlantic.

Shut out of British ports, Trippe pushed forward his plan to cross the Pacific to Asia with lucrative mail *and* passengers. All he needed was a bigger, long-range aircraft—bigger and farther-reaching than any flying boats already built by Sikorsky or Martin. Trippe never gave up. Like a bulldog, he just kept coming from different angles to take another bite until he got what he wanted. In 1936, with both the Atlantic and Pacific oceans still in his sights, he asked the major aircraft manufacturers for a larger, faster flying boat. Lockheed, Sikorsky, and Douglas passed. Martin offered a larger version of the M-130, the M-156. But Boeing asked for a time extension in order to make an extensive study.

Wellwood Beall, a design engineer for Boeing, had been making sketches in his spare time of a large flying boat that would use the huge wing Boeing had built for the XB-15 bomber. The new Wright engines, with a whopping 1,500 horsepower, gave plenty of leeway for frills. Along with a team of engineers, Boeing gave Beall approval to give it a try. The numbers were far better than Boeing or Pan Am expected, *and* it was beautiful! Pan Am signed a contract for six of the B-314s with an option for six more, and construction began at the Seattle plant.

In 1927, when Pan Am was in its infancy, Trippe hired a diminutive but formidable Dutchman, André Priester. He was made vice president of operations, maintenance, and engineering, and wore all three hats vigorously. Taking up residence in Seattle, he looked over Boeing's shoulder every step of the way, making constant demands and suggestions in the design and building of the new

B-314 cut-away model. *Courtesy of PAHF.*

plane. Priester was never wrong. Foremost in his mind was aircraft efficiency and safety, which made him a hero with crewmembers. He made sure that posted on many walls throughout Pan Am's offices were the words of *Captain A. G. Lamplugh*, chief underwriter and principal surveyor of British Aviation Insurance Company:

Aviation is not in itself inherently dangerous. But to an even greater extent than the sea, it is terribly unforgiving of any carelessness, incapacity, or neglect.

Thanks in great part to the persistent Priester, who relentlessly nagged the airplane and engine manufacturers to produce more efficient products, by 1939 Pan American had an international reputation for the best-built, best-maintained, safest airplanes, and the best-trained crews in the world.

In 1949, English aircraft manufacturer De Havilland announced the test flight of the *Comet*, the first jet-powered passenger plane— an ironic and unfortunate name because three of them fell apart in flight, killing everyone on board. Prior to the *Comet's* demise, Priester demonstrated a rarely witnessed sense of humor by sending Christmas cards to all the US airlines and aircraft builders. The card's only message read, "The British are coming."

In the air we were aviators, but on water we were sailors. Priester insisted that, like all sailors worth their salt, we each had to carry a knife, preferably along the lines of a Boy Scout knife with four blades. Most of us chose Swiss Army knives, some with as many as ten tools. If a crewmember reported for a flight and couldn't produce a knife, he was replaced and sent home with his pay docked. As a result, the chief pilot's clever secretary kept a supply in an unlocked desk drawer. Naturally, we called the knife the "Priester."

The Dutchman was keenly aware of the company's public image, insisting that each departure and arrival demonstrate a show of crew professionalism. Along with unbending uniform regulations, "show time" included the fanfare of crews marching to and from the airplanes in Bristol style: shoulders back, arms straight down, with eyes straight ahead. At virtually all of Pan Am's destinations, precise protocol was to be followed to the letter. Upon arrivals, before the march from the plane commenced, engineers were to give the maintenance log to the station foreman; radio operators were required to hand over the radio log to a radio mechanic, and the purser's instructions were to give the ship's papers to an operations clerk. Nothing more. Nothing less.

During one of his many "surprise" inspections, Priester was in San Francisco to witness the arrival of a B-314. He watched unnoticed from a second-story window of the Treasure Island Terminal Building as the crew began their disembarking march. His blood began a slow boil as he watched the engineers fall out of line to talk with a maintenance foreman. The radio operators began conversations with a radio mechanic, while the stewards chatted casually with the port steward. Priester's blood reached a full boil when the captain and co-pilot broke rank to greet their wives, leaving only the three junior pilots to complete the official march.

Furious, Priester stormed into the chief pilot's office, demanding that immediate, appropriate disciplinary action be taken. The next day the chief pilot, "Captain Jack" Tilton, called the entire crew back to Treasure Island where, in full uniform, they marched for two hours, back and forth from the empty dock to the terminal building. Word traveled fast. Marching protocol was never violated again—at least not from anywhere Priester witnessed.

After a few technical glitches were worked out, the Boeing 314 became a phenomenal success. Trippe opted for the six additional aircraft. Meanwhile, the British were still trying to build a seaplane that could profitably cross the Atlantic. With little immediate hope of acquiring the needed aircraft, Imperial Airways reached an agreement with Pan Am in 1937. The two companies would provide joint service between Bermuda and New York.

Two years later, Trippe finally won the battle for European routes, and on June 28, 1939, the Boeing 314 *Dixie Clipper* departed from Port Washington, New York, with twenty-two passengers. She flew the southern route to Horta in the Azores, to Lisbon, then on to Marseille. However, because WWII was now raging across Europe, the route was soon canceled. Meanwhile, the British were still desperate for a long-range aircraft in order to reach their far-flung territories. In a brilliant political and economic move, Trippe agreed to sell three of the new Pan Am Boeings to Imperial Airways, at considerable profit.

Discipline was just as rigid on the flight deck as it was on the ground. Leaving no doubt as to who was in full charge, each senior captain was issued a certificate designating him "Master of Ocean Flying Boats." They took it seriously.

Whenever we were wearing our Pan Am uniforms, casual conversation with fellow crewmembers was forbidden. I was called "Mister Kewin," or, if the captain didn't know my name, he referred to me as "Mister Engineer." After days of flying together, we all knew each other well, but on the flight deck, discipline and formality ruled.

During the war, Pan Am provided flight crews to both the army and navy. As a result, my duties and schedules varied. I might fly to Honolulu on a scheduled Pan Am flight before continuing to the South Pacific on a military flight, where the culture onboard and off was far more relaxed. Nicknames, jokes, and casual conversation were the norm, but we left our Pan Am uniforms in a closet at the Moana Hotel. In the event of capture by Japanese forces, and to avoid being mistakenly identified as spies, we wore military khaki uniforms and carried Geneva Convention ID cards.

When Pan Am crews prepared for departures, the dock signal was given, indicating all hatches were closed and stay ropes were removed. Only one cable remained attached to the back of the keel, which was when the captain called for the "Start Checklist." By then, all flight deck crews were wearing headsets, using workable microphones, allowing everyone to know what was happening without having to resort to hand signals.

Many of Pan Am's navigators came from shipping lines, professionally trained at maritime schools. At Pan Am's top-notch flight facilities in Dinner Key, Florida, and Alameda, California, navigators, radio operators, flight engineers, and pilots were carefully handpicked and trained. Most were cross-trained, qualifying them to take over other cockpit positions when needed.

Late afternoon departures were preferred for the advantage of nighttime celestial navigation. In clear weather, with night skies full of stars, navigators used an octant to measure the elevation of three specific stars. They were then carefully plotted, creating a small triangle on the navigator's chart, pinpointing the aircraft's position. Using these celestial markers, the navigator could determine both the location and speed of the aircraft. Similarly, in daylight, navigators took shots measuring the angle of the sun. Then, with precise instruments, an exact longitude and time would be entered on his chart.

At the time, celestial navigation was the best and most reliable system, but not without frequent educated guesses and judgment calls from the flight deck.

During unfavorable weather conditions, or whenever stars were not visible, "dead reckoning" was the alternative means of navigation. The navigator calculated the aircraft's position based on heading, speed, and the predicted wind. Because I find the term ominous, I've always preferred "deduced reasoning." Charles Lindbergh made his famous flight to Paris navigating purely by compass headings (magnetic) and forecast winds: dead reckoning, or deduced reasoning.

By 1943, we had radio direction finder equipment with which we could track the aircraft's position for the first 200 miles. For the remainder of the flight, the navigator plotted our progress with a series of star shots using his octant.

The reporting positions were longitude and latitude points, such as thirty-five degrees north latitude and 130 degrees west longitude. I drew up my calculations on a chart called the "howgozit" curve, which showed time horizontally and fuel vertically. Along with the flight plan, I plotted the forecast fuel and times on an upper line and the reserve fuel on a lower line. As we approached a reporting position, the navigator and I coordinated his position fix and my

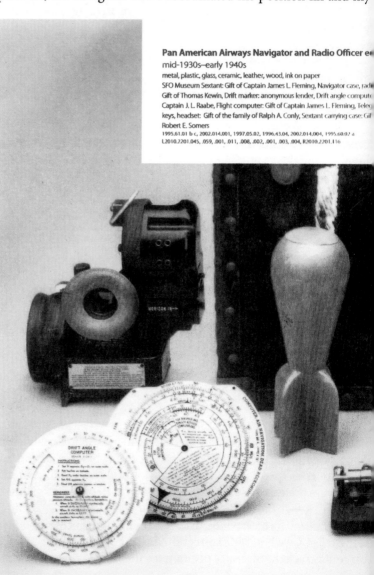

Pan American Airways Navigator and Radio Officer e◆
mid-1930s–early 1940s
metal, plastic, glass, ceramic, leather, wood, ink on paper
SFO Museum Sextant: Gift of Captain James L. Fleming, Navigator case, radi◆
Gift of Thomas Kewin, Drift marker: anonymous lender, Drift angle compute◆
Captain J. L. Raabe, Flight computer: Gift of Captain James L. Fleming, Tele◆
keys, headset: Gift of the family of Ralph A. Conly, Sextant carrying case: Gif◆
Robert E. Somers
1995.61.01 b c, 2002.014.001, 1997.05.02, 1996.43.04, 2002.014.004, 1995.60.02 a
L2010.2201.045, .059, .001, .011, .008, .002, .001, .003, .004, R2010.2201.116

fuel computations. Then, by putting those on the howgozit, we could readily see our progress.

With a solid overcast, the process of deduced reasoning could be enhanced with an accurate reading of the wind direction and velocity. One of the tools the navigator used was a drift meter, located at the aft end of his chart table. Resembling a submarine periscope in reverse, the drift meter had an eyepiece with a series of mirrors, allowing him a view of the ocean's surface. If the white caps of waves could be seen, a grid could be rotated until the waves moved parallel

PILOTS RADIOGRAM
NC-

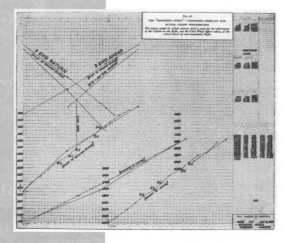

Howgozit chart.
Courtesy of
PAHF.

to lines on the grid. This observation allowed us to determine wind drift and calculate the movement of the aircraft based on heading and speed.

Another daylight tool was an aluminum dust or drift bomb, which was dropped from a tube in the left-wing tunnel. When it impacted on the sea, a shiny spot could be observed for five or six minutes. Similarly, at night we dropped a flare bomb. With a known drift angle, the magnetic heading was adjusted to keep the aircraft on track. For even more precision, we did what was called a double drift. The pilot turned the aircraft forty-five degrees port (left) and held that heading for a minute while the navigator took a drift reading. Then, the pilot would turn ninety degrees starboard (right) for another reading. Finally, he returned to the original compass heading. Using a specially designed round slide rule, the navigator was able to record accurate wind direction and velocity. In a word, we were hunting the wind.

The B-314 had the capacity to carry a useful load of 34,000 pounds of fuel, mail, cargo, and passengers. Every pound of fuel reduced income potential, so Flight Operations created what was called "long-range cruise," essentially meaning to fly as efficiently as possible. The most efficient speed was 110 percent of stall speed, but because that was difficult to fly, especially in turbulence, a compromise of 115 percent of stall speed was used. Stall speed is a function of weight—the higher the weight, the higher the stall speed—so the highest speed was reached at the top of the climb. On the B-314, as on other aircraft,

Boeing B-314
wing access
for in-flight
engine service.
Courtesy of
PAHF and
Thomas Kewin.

as fuel was consumed and as the weight decreased, we regularly reduced the power and the target speed. When we made the turn at Diamond Head and started our descent to Pearl Harbor, the engines slowed to about 1,400 rpm. With a geared propeller drive, the propeller would go down to about 800 rpm. At that reduced rpm, I could see the individual blades turning.

During the designing of the B-314, Priester insisted that Boeing install tunnels, or catwalks, in the wings. Rightfully, he believed that access to the engines during flight would contribute to safety. On one of my flights to Honolulu, about five hours out of San Francisco, the Number Three engine started running rough, even backfiring. When I enriched the fuel air mixture from my flight deck station, it smoothed out nicely, but that meant our ability to reach Honolulu could be jeopardized.

A check of the magnetos, a device that produces high-voltage current for distribution to the spark plugs, showed the right one had failed. I shut down the engine and feathered the prop, turning the blades to parallel the airflow so they would not continue to rotate. While the other engineer took over on the flight deck, I crawled down the wing tunnel to the Number Three engine with a spare magneto, tool bag, headset, and microphone. As a fire precaution, the engine was closed off from the tunnel by a two-piece, stainless steel clamshell cover with click latches for quick removal. To access the engine, I removed the clamshell and magneto covers. Using the interphone, I coached the other engineer on the flight deck to "bump" the start switch until the distributor finger was lined up with the Number One cylinder spark plug lead. Then I swapped the failed magneto for the new one. We un-feathered the prop and started the engine. It worked perfectly all the way to Honolulu.

The wing tunnels saved the day many times, proving once again Priester was right. My only problem was the tight fit. With my six-foot, two-inch frame, I always had scabs where my back scraped against the overhead wing ribs. My other problem was the persistent noise. It's no wonder I've worn hearing aids for most of my life.

Pan American Airways Boeing 314 flying boats moored at San Francisco Airport Seaplane Harbor, 1946. Courtesy of PAHF.

Thomas Kerwin, second from the right, stands with crew of the last scheduled Pacific Flying Boat Service. Courtesy of PAHF

Although we joked about our low pay, Pan Am paid the best salaries, and we all agreed the prestige of "Clipper glory" was compensation in itself, not to mention the added benefit of more time at home. My salary was $154 a month, the same as a Navy ensign at the time. Normal limits set by the Civil Aeronautics Bureau were eighty-five flight hours per month, but during the war they were raised to 120 hours. I usually flew more than one hundred hours, putting my hourly pay at about $1.50 an hour.

The last San Francisco arrival of a Pan Am flying boat was on April 8, 1946, the B-314 *American Clipper*, and I was one of the crewmembers. The company's publicity director, William Van Dusen, was there to take pictures of the passengers, crew, and aircraft. He sent press releases to newspapers all over the US. It made the full front page in Seattle, but was probably only a two-inch item on a back page in other US cities.

As my crew and I marched up the ramp, I broke protocol a few times looking back at *American Clipper*. She bore the aging signs of having faithfully served her company and her country during times of peace and war. But in my eyes, she was still beautiful.

Waiting for us with tears in his eyes was the maintenance foreman. "Shorty" Greenough was one of the first people hired at San Francisco in 1935. He had worked with the B-314s for seven years and loved the old birds.

Marching to the terminal building for the last time, we couldn't help noticing a nearby shiny, brand-new Lockheed Constellation decked in Pan Am colors. This new generation of Pan Am aircraft would decrease flight time to Hawaii from sixteen to a mere seven hours. They would carry more passengers and use less fuel. They would take off and land from runways built all over the world during the war.

Just as I'd had the good luck to work my first flight on Pan Am's most famous flying boat, the *China Clipper*—our "Sweet Sixteen"—so I was fortunate once again. This time, I delivered the last "boat" to San Francisco.

Shorty's eyes said it all. Everyone who'd proudly worn their uniform wings or had worked in any capacity on the Martins and Boeings loved them. Unbelievably, almost overnight, they'd become dinosaurs. The end of the great flying boat era was a hard reality to swallow. But what a ride it was!

Chin Yun Gi was part of a well-known family of "floating people." Amid the bustling waterfront of Hong Kong Harbor, where Pan Am flying boats were docked, she and hundreds of others wove their sampans through floating villages and markets, dodging pleasure yachts, tankers, and passenger liners.

Sampan Annie, standing in boat next to *Hong Kong Clipper*. SFO Museum Louis A. Turpen Aviation Museum and Library.

During the first Clipper arrival in 1936, Base Maintenance foreman "Shorty" Greenough spotted her and instantly knew that, along with a crew of other Chinese helpers, she was the right person for the job of tying up and securing the planes.

He was right. Whenever a Clipper arrived or departed, she would be alongside, maneuvering her craft as close as possible. Passing a line to the officer on the bow, she made sure that the breast and tail lines were firmly in place. Her skills and dedication to Pan Am quickly earned her the respect of the pilots and ground crew.

Barefooted, dressed in traditional black baggy shirt and pants and a bamboo "coolie" hat, she soon became affectionately known as Sampan Annie.

Because of sharp protuberances and corners on her sampan, Pan Am built her a brand new modified version. Designed to protect the Clippers, it included protective padding around the gunwales and improved steering mechanisms.

Annie's most cherished possession was a PAA Flight Engineer button, which she proudly wore to work, albeit sometimes upside down. After tending to the Clippers, accompanied by a gaggle of children and grandchildren, she collected every bit of leftover food from the Clippers' galleys for family feasts. She and her husband presided over their brood from an eighty-foot junk. Adding to the family's fishing fleet, each son received a forty-foot sampan when he married.

Dependable Annie was late only once, but she had a good excuse. She'd taken a few hours off to give birth to the most recent of eight children. Later that same day, the hefty Annie single-handedly hoisted the massive Clipper from a beached position where it was stuck.

The Long Way Way Home
A Flight into History

Ed Dover

CHAPTER 6

Reprinted with permission from Ed Dover's book, *The Long Way Home,* publisher Ed Dover (revised edition November 22, 2010).

The Adventure Begins—December 1, 1941

W hen Capt. Robert Ford and his ten-man crew boarded the Boeing B-314 (NC 18606) at Treasure Island on December 1, 1941, for a routine commercial flight to Auckland, New Zealand, little did they know they were embarking on a flight into history.

Captain Ford. *Courtesy of PAHF.*

One of the crew, First Officer Tom White, had joined the flight at the last minute when Ford's regularly scheduled first officer, John Mack, was unable to get to Treasure Island in time for the scheduled 3:00 p.m. departure. Mack reported the next day to work the B-314, NC 18602. He would catch up with Ford at Honolulu for the flight south to New Zealand. Tom White would return to San Francisco on NC 18606. Rounding out the rest of the crew were Second Officer Roderick Norman Brown, Third Officer James G. Henricksen, Fourth Officer John Delmer Steers, First Flight Engineer Homans K. "Swede" Rothe, Second Flight Engineer John B. Parrish, First Flight Radio Officer Oscar Hendrickson, Flight Steward Barney Sawicki, and Assistant Flight Steward Verne C. Edwards.

Also accompanying Ford on this flight was Chief Flight Radio Officer Jack Poindexter, who was on board only as far as San Pedro, just far enough to check out new radio equipment that had recently been installed on the Clippers. Another flight radio officer, Harry Strickland, would join the crew at San Pedro for the remainder of the trip. When Strickland failed to show up for the flight to Honolulu, Poindexter was all but shanghaied by Ford to continue on to Auckland. Pan Am required two flight officers for each operating position on the Boeing Clippers.

Some confusion arises when reviewing the Pan American Airways (PAA) images. The archives have images of the *California Clipper* sporting both NC 18602 and NC 18609 registration numbers. When PAA transferred the older NC 18602 to the Atlantic Division, they replaced it with the newer NC 18609. Marketing decided to name the new clipper *California Clipper*. However, within months the Pacific Division permanently changed the name to the *Pacific Clipper*. The US Navy requisitioned *Pacific Clipper* (NC 18609) in 1942 to carry wartime VIPs and priority cargo through-

out the Pacific. After the war, Universal Airlines purchased NC 18609 in 1946. In 1950, a storm damaged it beyond repair and Universal Airlines subsequently salvaged the once proud *Pacific Clipper* for parts. It was a sad end for the magnificent aircraft.

Once on board, Ford reached for his flight case. He removed a flat, sealed envelope and carefully placed it inside the breast pocket of his uniform jacket. The envelope had large black letters stamped on it: "PLAN A—TOP SECRET—FOR CAPTAIN'S EYES ONLY." It was to be opened only when (and the emphasis was on *when*, not *if*) hostilities began.

And so, on December 2, Ford and his full crew embarked on the longest leg of their flight plan, 2,400 miles across the Pacific to Honolulu.

In Warm Springs, Georgia, following an urgent telephone call from Secretary of State Cordell Hull, President Franklin D. Roosevelt cut short his vacation plans and boarded the presidential train for a hurried return to Washington. (New York Times, *Tuesday, December 2, 1941*).

Somewhere between Hitukappu Bay in the Kurile Islands and Lat 40°N, Long 170°W a Japanese task force consisting of six carriers, two battleships, three cruisers, and several destroyers and tankers, under the command of Vice Admiral Chuichi Nagumo, steamed steadily toward the rendezvous point from which they would head south towards Hawaii, maintaining strict radio silence.

At noon on December 3, Ford and his crew had arrived at Pearl Harbor. They checked in at the Moana Hotel in Waikiki where they relaxed, enjoyed the pleasant amenities of the Hawaiian Islands, and refreshed themselves for the next stage of their journey. The flight would take them south via Canton Island, Suva, Fiji, and Noumea, New Caledonia, to Auckland, New Zealand.

Seven hundred miles northwest of Oahu, Admiral Nagumo's task force proceeded at reduced speed through a winter storm that stirred the North Pacific. While the storm had forced them to slow to a more cautious pace, the cloud cover was a welcome sight: It would ensure protection against early detection by any American aerial patrols that might stray into the area. And the strict radio silence imposed upon the fleet made detection by that means impossible.

On December 4, the *Pacific Clipper* departed Pearl Harbor for the flight to Auckland. Having crossed the International Date Line between Canton Island and Suva, they lost one day on the calendar, arriving at Noumea on December 7. It was December 6 at Pearl Harbor.

The War Begins—December 8, Noumea time —December 7 at Pearl Harbor

Prior to departing Noumea for Auckland, they took on one more crewmember. Radio Officer Eugene Leach, who had been on temporary ground duty at Noumea, was now assigned to proceed to Auckland, where he would work on radio gear. When he joined Ford and his crew, Poindexter put him to work at the radio desk. About two hours out of Auckland, Leach decided to tune in a commercial broadcast station in hopes of listening to music. Instead, the voice of an Auckland announcer came in loud and clear:

". . . no confirmation from the American Consulate in Auckland at this time, but it appears that Japanese naval forces have launched a surprise attack on the American naval base at Pearl Harbor on the Hawaiian Island of Oahu. Unconfirmed reports indicate that at least two waves of bombers have destroyed or disabled a great number of naval vessels and have also attacked and severely damaged Army and Air Force installations at Schofield Barracks and Hickam Field. We are attempting to obtain details from the American Consulate, but all communications are subject to priority delays. Please stand by and we will bring you the latest developments as they become available."

Immediately, Leach informed Captain Ford, who knew exactly what to do. He opened the Plan A document and followed instructions by continuing to Auckland, where he conferred with Pan Am Station Manager Bill Mullahey (see chapter 4). The Plan A document contained few details except to remove all identifying insignia from the aircraft and remain in Auckland until further orders came from

Pan Am's New York headquarters, relayed through the coded diplomatic channels of the American Consulate. A heavy flow of war traffic created a six-day delay. Not until December 14 did Ford receive the message he was waiting for.

Captain Ford and Verne White, Auckland's chief mechanic, were instructed to take on board as many spare B-314 engine parts as possible, then return to Noumea and evacuate all Pan American personnel and dependents to Gladstone, Australia. From there, the evacuees would be taken to Sydney for steamship transport to the United States. In addition, Ford was ordered to add the Noumea mechanics to his crew and proceed westbound under radio silence as best he could—all the way to New York. Without navigation charts—only with atlases "borrowed" from the Auckland public library—the remaining round-the-world route would be a true seat-of-the-pants journey across *terra incognita*.

A Hazardous Night Takeoff from Auckland —December 16, 1941

Flying through the night, they arrived at Noumea in the early morning hours of December 17. Station Manager Folger Athearn had heard the Clipper making its unscheduled approach and was anxiously waiting at the dock for Ford's news—news he knew wouldn't be good. When Ford instructed Athearn to initiate the immediate evacuation of all Pan Am employees and their dependents,

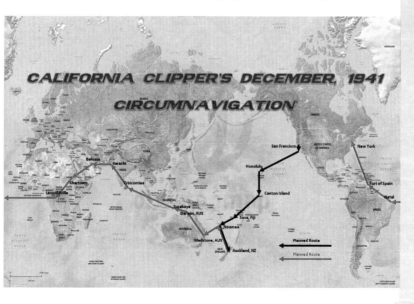

Map of Ford's flight. Courtesy of Ed Dover.

a frantic scramble ensued. Two hours later, refueled and ready to leave with the dazed passengers and Noumea mechanics on board, *Pacific Clipper* took off for Gladstone.

Soon after arriving at Gladstone, Ford discovered there was no 100-octane aviation fuel available; they would have to continue on with only the fuel remaining in the tanks. The captain and his crew would head northwest to the port of Darwin, Australia. From there, the globe-girdling mission would take them across seas and lands where none of the crew had ever flown. After departing Australia, they would have no certainty of finding fuel, aircraft servicing, or even food.

A Very Close Call—December 18, 1941

Shortly after dawn, they departed Darwin for the next unscheduled leg of the journey: the Dutch airbase at Surabaya, Indonesia. By late afternoon, they were about seventy-five miles from their destination when they were intercepted by four Dutch fighter planes. Never having seen such a large aircraft before, some of the Dutch pilots were eager to shoot it down, but radio instructions from their commander instructed them to simply follow the enormous flying boat, making sure it didn't present any visible threat to the airbase.

Ford made a very slow, low approach to Surabaya. When he saw the harbor was crowded with ships, without a suitable landing area, he elected to land just outside the breakwater and taxi in to the harbor. After coming ashore, Ford spoke with the Dutch

Pacific Clipper at Trincomalee December 1941. Courtesy of PAHF.

commander and learned that, by setting down outside the breakwater, they had landed in the middle of a minefield.

When Ford inquired about the availability of 100-octane fuel, the commander informed him that none was available. The small supply of aviation fuel on hand was reserved for the Dutch fighter planes. He could, however, offer Ford regular 90-octane auto gas. Ford knew that anything less than 100-octane could cause backfiring and cylinder damage if used in the high compression Wright engines for any extended time, but he had little choice. The flight from Darwin had used up almost all of their fuel. It was auto gas or nothing. Ford conferred with flight engineer Swede Rothe, and they reluctantly but mutually agreed to take the lower octane fuel.

It was late the next day, December 19, before they were able to depart Surabaya for their next destination, the British base at Trincomalee on the island of Ceylon (now Sri Lanka). When they tried to adjust the engines for a long-range fuel mixture, the engines experienced severe backfiring, which forced the Clipper to remain at a lower altitude for the night crossing of the Bay of Bengal. Flying through stormy weather, they navigated strictly by dead reckoning. A heavy overcast obscured any view of the sky, preventing them from using the far more reliable method of celestial navigation. It was a long, slow, turbulent ride across the bay. When dawn finally broke, the exhausted crew was alarmed to realize their altitude was only 300 feet above the water. Moments later, with visibility improving, John Mack spotted a strange shape rising out of the sea in front of them. Suddenly it became clear. The apparition was a Japanese submarine surfacing directly in their flight path, and the Clipper was too close to change course. Forced to fly directly over it, they watched helplessly as submarine crewmembers rushed to man a deck gun, swing it around, and take aim at the Clipper. Ford slammed the throttles to full power, hauled back on the control wheel, and headed for the nearest cloud cover. Just as they penetrated the low cloud base, a sudden flash of light signaled that the Japanese had fired at them. *Pacific Clipper's* crew tensed for the impact, but nothing happened. The shot had missed them, and they were still climbing.

Later, at a safe distance and a higher altitude, Captain Ford descended once again to observe the sea. Relying on the maps borrowed from Auckland's public library, all on board kept watch for the coastal port of Trincomalee.

After an uneventful landing, followed by eventful British protocol, Ford was ushered into the office of the British commander. Ford reported the Clipper's encounter with the Japanese submarine and inquired about the availability of 100-octane fuel. The British commander assured Ford that the correct grade of aviation fuel was available. In addition, the British would provide Clipper's navigators with up-to-date charts for their continued flights through British India, the Near East, and Africa, including Leopoldville, Belgian Congo, where Pan American was starting up a base.

Christmas Eve—December 24, 1941

Six days later, after delays in obtaining the promised British navigation charts, Ford and his crew departed for the next stop, Karachi, India. Thirty minutes into the flight, *Pacific Clipper* was shaken by a loud explosion. The flying boat yawed right, and Ford instinctively applied corrective rudder and aileron. As he did so, he glanced out his portside window toward the engines. Johnny Mack turned to inspect the engines on the starboard side. A wide, black swath of oil was streaming back from the Number Three engine.

"Number three's lost oil pressure!" Swede Rothe called from the engineer's station. "Cutting off fuel flow, feathering Three!"

Mack watched as the big Hamilton propeller slowed and stopped with the blades slanted edgewise into the air stream, then he switched off the magnetos for Number Three.

"Jocko!" Ford called to John Parrish, who was standing next to the engineer's desk. "Get up to the dome and see if you can make out what's happened to number three."

Parrish hurried through the hatch to the rear compartment and climbed the short ladder. Glancing out of the dome, he could see the problem.

"It looks like we've blown a jug," Parrish reported. "It's a real mess out there."

Ford swung the Clipper around in a 180-degree turn. "Well, that does it. With possible complications of an oil leak, we'll have to return to Trincomalee."

Half an hour later, they were circling back over the harbor at Trincomalee. As soon as *Pacific Clipper* was secured to the seaplane dock and all engines were shut down, Swede Rothe and Jocko Parrish climbed out on top of the wing to inspect the damaged engine.

"We've blown number six cylinder on the number three engine," Rothe reported to Ford. "Ten studs are broken. We're going to have to draw those broken studs out before we can replace the cylinder from our spare parts. Better figure on at least two days to get the job done. Merry Christmas!"

It took all of that day and the better part of Christmas Day for the crew to repair the damaged engine using spare parts they were carrying from the Auckland base.

December 26th:

With the engine repaired, once again they departed Trincomalee for Karachi. Upon landing at Karachi Swede Rothe informed Ford that during a routine engine inspection they had discovered that the Number Three engine had a malfunctioning propeller pitch control. It would take the better part of a day to repair it.

On the morning of December 27th, they departed Karachi for Bahrain. Following a smooth flight they discovered that there was no 100-octane fuel available. They would have to make do with auto gas once again. Fortunately, the flight from Trincomalee was short enough so that they needed only to top off with the auto gas. This still led to some backfiring as the high compression engines voiced their objections to the lower rated fuel. Cutting across Saudi Arabia at 10,000 feet they soon found themselves the target of ground based rifle fire as they flew directly over the great Mosque at Mecca and thousands of angry pilgrims demonstrated their objection to this aerial invasion of their sacred land. The rifle fire could not reach them at their altitude and they continued without further incident to their landing on the Nile at Khartoum.

Ford found that the seaplane channel on the Nile, while long enough to land on, was too short for the takeoff run the Boeing required. They had to measure an additional distance on the river. This took the better part of another day.

They departed Khartoum on New Year's Day—January 1st, 1942.

Ten hours and twenty-three minutes out of Khartoum, Ford lined up as best he could on the winding Congo River and eased the big ship onto the surface at Leopoldville, Belgian Congo (now Kinshasa, Democratic Republic of the Congo). As the Boeing slowed and settled, Ford felt the tug of the river current. He had thought it to be a sluggish current when viewed from the air, but it was much stronger than he'd expected, running at about six knots. They would require secure anchorage.

Pan American was just beginning to build its African bases at the beginning of the war, and Leopoldville was still in its early phases of construction when *Pacific Clipper* made its unexpected arrival. Even though facilities were somewhat limited, the supply of 100-octane aviation fuel was plentiful, *and* there was the Grand Hotel. Ford made

Pacific Clipper treetop level over Africa. Courtesy of PAHF.

arrangements for refueling for the next day. Then he and his crew went ashore to snatch what sleep they could at the hotel. The climate was the hottest and muggiest they had experienced so far. Added to the discomfort of humidity and heat, mosquito netting over their beds did little to protect them from swarms of the biting insects.

Taking Off from the Congo River —New Year's Day—January 1, 1942

The leg from Leopoldville to Natal, Brazil, would be the longest flight leg any Clipper had ever covered: 3,100 nautical miles, most of it over open ocean. There would be no place to refuel if they went below the allowable reserve supply. If they had to use up the reserve, they would have to consider a forced landing at sea. The Boeing might survive the landing, but it was never designed for extended surface operations on open seas. Ocean waves and wind would most likely make short work of the ship, and they would then find themselves adrift in the inflatable life rafts, hoping for a rescue that might or might not come. The length of the proposed flight with likely headwinds, plus conditions for a safe landing were all serious considerations, but the biggest unknown was how much fuel to take aboard. While there were no passengers, the collection of spare engine parts, stacked and scattered throughout the lower passenger cabin, created additional weight.

"Well, Skipper," Rothe replied, "it's possible to load as much as 5,100 gallons of fuel on board. But that would put us about 2,000 pounds over gross, even *without* any passengers or spare parts. If we were taking off in a cold climate with real low temperatures, I'd say it would be no problem, but this damned heat plays hell with density altitude. We'd need a helluva long takeoff channel to get off."

Ford pondered Rothe's words. "This river is pretty long. There's not really any high terrain to clear after takeoff. What do you think?"

Rothe shrugged. "If we have no engine glitches and if we can get off within the full-power parameters, I'd say let's go for it."

"Okay then, you get those tanks topped brim-full, and we'll get out of this hell hole as soon as you're done."

It was midday before all the fuel was loaded. Eager to get under way, the crew had come on board earlier, but the stifling weather made the flight deck feel like a Turkish bath. The sooner they could get to high altitude with cooler air circulating through the cabin, the better they would like it. But before they could go, Ford had to consider one other factor that would affect the takeoff.

When they had landed the day before, Ford had noted the strong current running in the Congo. The downstream flow was about six knots. Also downwind, a light breeze was blowing at about four knots. He could elect to take off upstream, against the wind, but that would give him a six-knot drag from the current. This could pose a problem when it came time to haul the big flying boat off the water. On the other hand, if he took off downstream, he would lose the four-knot airspeed advantage, but pick up a six-knot push from the current. After considering the alternatives, he made his decision.

"Okay, Johnny," Ford said to Mack. "We taxi upstream as far as the next bend in the river. Then we take off downstream. With this heat, I'm thinking we'd get a better advantage from the six-knot current than from the four-knot headwind."

"Downstream it is then," Mack agreed.

With the temperature hovering at 100 degrees, the crew was wringing wet with sweat as they started their pre-flight checklists. When all engines were running and the bow lines were cast off, Ford shoved the throttles forward, swung around, and headed upstream. Reaching the first bend, he swung around again. Immediately, he could feel the current carrying them downstream.

"Let's not waste time, Swede. Full takeoff power, NOW!"

The engines roared. Aided by the six-knot current, *Pacific Clipper* surged forward. Ford concentrated his gaze far ahead downriver to the drop-off of the Congo Gorges, a series of treacherous rapids and waterfalls, tumbling through a jumbled maze of rocks and canyons. They would have to be airborne well before reaching that drop-off point. If not . . . Ford preferred not to think about it.

Ford pressed his left hand on the throttles, pushing hard against the full power stops. His right hand grasped the yoke, and his eyes concentrated on the river ahead as he mentally measured the rapidly decreasing distance to the gorge. Twenty seconds went by. Thirty seconds. Still no liftoff. The surface of the river was just as close as ever. Ford glanced quickly at the airspeed indicator. It read seventy knots, the design-rated landing/stall speed. As the airspeed needle crept above that mark, he gently brought the yoke back. The Clipper's bow rose above the horizon, but it did not break off the water. He pushed the yoke forward again and could see the edge of the gorge 1,700 yards away. More speed, he needed more speed to break the suction. He kept the nose down, hoping to build up the airspeed.

Fifty seconds now. Sixty. Seventy. Then he made a crucial decision: If they didn't break off in another twenty seconds, he would pull back three engines, but keep number one at full power. Its torque would swing the Boeing around, and they could head back upstream.

All eyes on the flight deck were fixed on the rapidly approaching gorge. No one uttered a word. Ford adjusted his grip on the throttles. He flexed his left hand—and at that moment, NC 18602 came off the water.

Sighs of relief were audible, but it was a momentary reprieve. *Pacific Clipper* barely had flying speed, and they were not climbing at all. They were only hovering a few feet off the surface and were still headed toward the gorge.

"Ninety-one seconds," Rothe called from the engineer's station. "That's past max time for full power. Can we pull it back now?"

"No way!" Ford called back. "Keep those throttles to the stops. We're not out of this yet!"

"Okay, but the cylinder head temps are over redline! We could blow at any time!"

Ford knew how much danger they were in but did not reply. To himself he thought, Hell! We'll either blow up or hit those rocks. Either way we're dead. Might as well die trying. And he kept his hand hard against the throttles.

Gingerly he tested the yoke, attempting to find a balance between pulling back too far and risking a stall. At the same time, he tried to maintain just enough nose-down attitude in order to build up the airspeed without settling back onto the river.

The moment they passed the rim of the gorge, the river dropped away into the rocky defile; downward-tumbling water turned to white foam as it crashed against the boulder-strewn bottom. Without the cushioning of "ground effect" (being only a few feet above the water's surface), *Pacific Clipper* began descending into the gorge. Within seconds, they had dropped into the confines of the narrow canyon, still not far above the water. Separation from the river's surface at least allowed Ford to drop the nose a little more and gradually the airspeed began to pick up.

"Eighty-five knots," Mack called out.

Okay, Ford figured, that gives us about five knots to play with to get some climb out of this baby. Gently, he exerted enough backpressure on the yoke to raise the nose and drop the airspeed to eighty knots.

"Rate of climb ten feet a minute, up!" Mack exclaimed. "Twenty feet, up! Fifty feet, up! We're going to make it!"

"We're not out of the woods yet, Johnny," Ford cautioned. "Look up ahead there."

Directly ahead, the gorge took a curve to the right. They were still below the edge of the precipice and a rocky ledge loomed before them. "There seems to be room to make a shallow turn and follow the canyon."

"Yeah, as long as we don't bank too far. We're still marginal for a stall."

Ford watched the approaching curve and mentally gauged the point at which to begin a gentle turn. As they reached that point, he gently applied pressure to the wheel, turning it to the right, while at the same time, feeding in light pressure on the right rudder pedal. The wheel would not move. He increased pressure. The yoke would not budge. He could move it forward and back, but he could not get it to turn. With no aileron movement and with only a slight amount of right rudder, the ship skidded left.

"Now what the hell is wrong?" he exclaimed. "Hey, Swede, we've got no aileron control! The damn wheel won't budge! What gives?"

Swede Rothe made a quick assessment: "The aileron cables must be jammed. Hang on! I'll check it out."

Leaping from his seat, he raced to the starboard hatch leading into the wing. He opened it, peered into the tunnel, and saw the problem immediately. Looking along the catwalk tunnel, he could see that it had a tilt to it, only slight, but noticeable to his trained eye. Then he turned his attention to the aileron cable running through the channels in the wing. In a matter of seconds, he understood the problem. At a point where the cable went through a pulley, it was clamped tightly between the groove of the pulley wheel and the pulley housing. Quickly he returned to his station.

"Skipper, the aileron cables are jammed in their pulleys because the wing is flexing. We're going to have to get up into cooler air before those pulleys will free up."

As Ford digested the report from Rothe, he was, at the same time, trying to improvise a way to make the big ship follow the twists and turns of the gorge. After quick experimentation, he found he could use the rudder pedal by itself to skid around the turns. Each time he applied right rudder, the ship would skid left and the right wing would dip down. Conversely, it worked the same when he attempted the left rudder. Guiding the huge Boeing only with the use of rudder pedals, Ford followed the curves of the gorge. Airspeed was just above stall, but they were gaining about fifty feet per minute.

Slowly, they finally reached enough height to put them above the surrounding terrain. It seemed a very long time before Ford was able to ease up on the yoke and build more airspeed, but at last, they climbed to a safe altitude. Ford called to Rothe to throttle back to normal cruise climb. The four engines had been held at full power for a full three minutes—far longer than the engineers at Wright had ever designed them to perform.

"By God, I don't want to try that again any time soon!" Rothe exclaimed to no one in particular.

The crew's tension eased as *Pacific Clipper* approached its normal cruising altitude, but Ford remained keenly alert, listening carefully to the engines. Finally satisfied the engines had not suffered any damage from the extended time at full power, he relaxed, but he knew it had been a very close call.

Getting back to normal on this very abnormal flight assignment, Ford called to Rod Brown for a compass heading to Natal, Brazil. As was customary, the navigator jotted the heading calculations onto a small slip of paper and taped it to the brow of the instrument panel. Following Brown's numbers, Ford turned the Clipper westward and headed toward the South Atlantic for the longest and, potentially, the most risky leg of the journey.

Twenty-three hours and thirty-five minutes after safely crossing the Atlantic Ocean, with only two hours of reserve fuel remaining, they landed at Natal. Once the Boeing was secured to the Pan American seaplane dock, the crew mutually agreed to keep the stopover as brief as possible. The finish line of their odyssey was in sight, and they were eager to reach it.

Following refueling and inspection by the Natal ground mechanics, Ford and his crew immediately departed for the next Pan Am base at Port-of-Spain, Trinidad. Thirteen hours later, they glided gently onto the seaplane channel. It was 3:00 a.m. They had been on the ship for more than forty hours since leaving Leopoldville.

Pacific Clipper had come all the way from Auckland with no identifying aircraft markers, always under complete radio silence, often forced to use low-grade fuel. She had been the target of a Japanese submarine, hostile Muslims, and a near-attack by Dutch fighter pilots. For finding their way during the first part of the mission, the crew had relied only on atlas books borrowed from the Auckland library. They had navigated mostly by visible landmarks during daylight hours and often by dead reckoning at night. Time and again, they had been plagued by mechanical failures, overcoming each one with ingenuity, clear thinking, and perseverance. The superb aviators of *Pacific Clipper* had done the impossible, taking off on the Congo River, traversing the treacherous gorge. Captain Ford and his crew had spent most of their ground time sleeping onboard the aircraft in uncomfortable, often stifling conditions, never knowing where or when food would be available. They had endured hardships few airline crews would ever experience. For nineteen days, no one—not Pan Am Operations, not the US military, and certainly not their families—knew where they were, or if they were alive or dead.

The Home Stretch—January 5, 1942

At two o'clock in the afternoon, they boarded *Pacific Clipper* at Port-of Spain, Trinidad, for the final leg of their globe-circling adventure. Flying through the night over the Amazon basin and the West Indies, at fourteen hours and forty-five minutes into the flight, Ford decided it was time to break radio silence. Jack Poindexter set up the transmitter and receiver on the local control channel. Ford pressed the button on his microphone:

"*Laguardia Tower, Laguardia Tower—Pan American Clipper NC 18602, inbound from Auckland, New Zealand. Captain Ford reporting. Due to arrive Pan American Marine Terminal Laguardia in seven minutes. Over.*"

The unexpected radio call stunned Pan Am Operations at the LaGuardia Marine Terminal. The news was then relayed to Pan Am's transatlantic manager and public relations director. They, in turn, notified Army Intelligence and US Immigration Service that Pan Am Clipper NC 18602 was inbound. No one else was aware that an utterly remarkable, nearly unbelievable chapter in aviation history was coming to a conclusion.

Epilogue

Other Pan American Clippers were also caught out along the line on December 7. They, too, had followed their "Plan A" orders, but none of their journeys returning to home base flew so far, for as long, and with as many challenges as the heroic crew of the *Pacific Clipper*.

Several years into the post-war era, the records Pan Am's flying boats had set would be eclipsed by new generations of land-based commercial airliners. By then, all the B-314s would be gone, but *Pacific Clipper's* astounding feats would remain embedded in the minds of Bob Ford and every member of his extraordinary crew. Their epic stories—the stuff of legends—would feed the fertile imaginations of their children, grandchildren, and future generations.

Rescue from Noumea

Merry Athearn Barton

CHAPTER 7

W hen I was a girl of five, the United States and Japan went to war. At the time, I lived with my parents and brother in the small capital of Noumea, New Caledonia, where my father, Folger Athearn, was Pan American's station manager. The island chain of New Caledonia is a French collectivity located about 1,000 miles east of Brisbane, Australia, and 1,000 miles west of Fiji.

The *Pacific Clipper* (civil registration NC 18602) departed from Noumea on schedule, en route to Auckland on the morning of December 8, 1941. In Honolulu, on the east side of the International Date Line, the date was December 7—a date described by President Roosevelt as "a day of infamy" when asking Congress to declare war on Japan. Months prior, Pan Am President Juan Trippe had strongly suspected that war between Japan and the US was imminent. As a precaution, he directed Pacific Division Operations to provide each Pacific captain with envelopes containing instructions if the unthinkable occurred. The Top Secret "Plan A" instructions were clear:

"Normal return route canceled. Proceed as follows: Strip all company markings, registration numbers and identifiable insignia from exterior surfaces. Proceed **westbound** *soonest your discretion to avoid hostilities and deliver NC 18602 to Marine Terminal La Guardia Field New York. Good luck."*

In other words, in order to reach New York, *Pacific Clipper* could not fly across the Pacific Ocean.

Meanwhile, aboard *Pacific Clipper*, Captain Robert Ford was in command of a crew of eleven with twelve passengers. Two hours out of Noumea, Radio Operator Eugene Leach picked up the voice of a New Zealand newscaster announcing the US Navy fleet at Pearl Harbor had been attacked by Japanese bombers. The unflappable Ford immediately removed the envelope from the breast pocket of his

uniform jacket, silenced the radio, posted watches in the navigator's blister in the roof of the Boeing, and drew his pistol. But nothing happened. Two hours later, he made a normal landing at Auckland.

After the passengers deplaned, Station Manager Bill Mullahey advised Captain Ford to sit tight. Nine tense days passed before New York headquarters finally ordered NC 18602 to depart for Noumea, where he was ordered to pick up Pan Am employees and their dependents. From there, he would proceed westbound toward Australia.

Amid the torpid climes of Noumea, nothing unusual was taking place on that early morning of December 17. It was as if a war wasn't even happening. The townspeople were going about their normal slow-paced lives. My mother, Marion Whitaker Athearn, and our half-French, half -Caledonian housekeeper, Eileen, were preparing food for a luau luncheon. Hanging out with them in the kitchen, I spoke with Eileen in the French I'd been learning at school. By then, it was normal for me to speak in English or French. I had no idea that other children my age, living back in the States, were not bilingual.

The luau would include a few of my mother's Pan Am friends, plus any Caledonians, or kanak, who might wander by. The kanak would get lunch, and the ladies would be serenaded by harmonic voices and ukulele tunes. Relaxing in the shade of breadfruit trees, everyone would relish in the island's favorite dish, bougna (steamed chicken, fish, taro, and coconut milk, wrapped in banana leaves).

As was his custom, Daddy had gone to work before dawn that day. Pan Am had hired him in April of 1941, after being trained at Treasure Island in San Francisco; then for six months he'd been stationed on Canton Atoll. His training, innate people skills, and

Merry Athearn's mother, smiling in foreground, and friends. *Courtesy of Merry Athearn Barton.*

experience well qualified him for the many hats he wore in New Caledonia. Among other responsibilities, my father orchestrated the arrivals and departures of the Clippers and oversaw local hires, as well as the Pan Am expatriate employees, who like us, had come from other countries.

Daddy was also responsible for providing layover accommodations for Clipper passengers and crews. In those days, there wasn't a single first-class hotel on the island, but anchored half a mile out of the bay was a dazzling twenty-stateroom motor yacht. Built in New York in 1920, it was christened *Lyndonia* by its original owner, Cyrus Curtiss. Pan Am purchased it in 1939, renamed it the *Southern Seas,* and converted it to the standards of a modern five-star hotel. While luxuriating onboard the three-deck, Jacobean/Tudor-style yacht, I imagined Clipper passengers feeling like pampered millionaires, as indeed many were.

While Mother and Eileen were preparing bougna, I stepped out onto our lanai (veranda). In my eyes, Noumea was a magical place to live. Everything seemed right with the world as I looked down at the bay where a dozen small boats bobbed on the tranquil sea. I couldn't see the dock, but I knew that was where the magnificent Boeing 314s tied up. I sighed. Waiting for the Clippers' return seemed eternities to a girl my age.

Soon after my family settled into life in Noumea, Daddy unfolded a map of the Pacific, showing my older brother Jerry and me the route the Clippers flew to New Caledonia.

"They originate here," Daddy said, putting his finger on San Francisco. "After stopping in Los Angeles, they come all the way across the Pacfric to Honolulu, Canton, and Fiji before continuing on to Noumea and finally to Auckland." Jerry and I followed his finger across the map, admiring our father's worldly knowledge.

There were few telephones in those days, so when the luau food was ready, my mother sent Eileen on foot to let everyone know the time they should gather at the usual shady spot. I can't remember where my seven-year-old brother had gone. Probably he was climbing coconut trees or doing other things boys did on a tropical island. Except for a vague awareness about the war, everything was as normal as apple pie, or bougna.

That normalcy changed in a heartbeat when my father came bursting through the front door. He was out of breath, and the look on his face told us he didn't have good news.

Immediately concerned, Mother asked, "What is it, Folger?"

"Listen," he said, pointing across the bay. "Can you hear it? The Clipper is coming in right *now!*"

My mother hesitated only a moment before responding, "How unusual."

"Exactly," Daddy said in an ominous tone. "This is an unscheduled arrival, and there was no radio message about the change. They must be flying under radio silence, or else they would have notified us. Something is very, very wrong."

With her usual calm, yet ready to spring into action, Mother asked, "What should we do, Folger?"

"Stand by," Daddy ordered in his resonating Gregory Peck voice. "I have to get back to the dock."

"I'll find Jerry!" I chimed in, happy to be a volunteer in this exciting emergency.

"You'll stay right here, Merry Athearn!" Mother commanded. "Eileen will be back soon. She can go find your brother."

Moments later Eileen rushed in the door with Jerry on her heels.

"*Mon Dieu, Madame! C'est terrible!*"

"English, Eileen. In English, please!"

"Le cleeper! Eet come now! Kanak afraid bombs come to Noumea! I think no luau today."

Just as Eileen stated the obvious, we heard the roar of *Pacific Clipper's* engines setting down in the channel.

Looking sternly at Jerry, who was still trying to process the news, and then at me, Mother calmly said, "I think the war must be escalating, but that's only a guess until your father gets back to us."

Looking directly at Eileen, in a warm voice, my mother said, "In case we are leaving, I want to thank you for all your help and kindness. You're like a member of our family . . . but now you must go to your real family."

Eileen gave a knowing smile to my mother before embracing Jerry and me in hard, kanak-style hugs. "*Je t'aimes, mes enfants. Au revoir.*" And then she was gone.

Merry Athearn in her wool traveling suit; photo taken by her father. *Courtesy of Merry Athearn Barton.*

The next two hours were pandemonium. Daddy was far too busy with the Clipper to come back up the hill to our house. Instead, a Pan Am employee delivered our instructions: "Prepare to leave immediately with only one suitcase per person. Come to the dock for tender boarding to the aircraft ASAP."

Worried that the other Pan Am expats might not have been notified about the impending evacuation, my mother jumped into our car and raced off to tell as many as she could find.

Young as we were, Jerry and I understood that time was of the essence, so off to our bedrooms we hurried to sort out what belongings would go with us and what would stay behind. When my mother returned in a dusty screech of brakes, Jerry and I were packed with one suitcase each, literally ready to fly. There was no time for the luxury of a shower, so my beautiful, take-charge mother quickly threw off her perspiration-soaked, island-print dress for a smart-looking traveling suit, then she turned to me.

"War or not, evacuation or not, you're traveling in proper Pan Am style, young lady."

Pulling from my closet the navy blue wool suit I'd worn nine months earlier for our journey to New Caledonia, she instructed, "Put this on. Oh, and don't forget the gloves and hat." Normally, she would have said "please," but this situation was far from normal.

I wondered what would become of the clothes and toys I was leaving behind, but mostly I was anxious about where we were going and what would become of Eileen, my classmates, and all the kanak friends we'd made. I was pretty sure they wouldn't be boarding the Clipper with my family and me.

Daddy was up to his eyeballs dealing with last-minute details when we hastily arrived at the dock. Captain Ford and his crew were lined up in company-required formation when the one-bell signal rang. The ground crew completed refueling, mechanical checklists, and last-minute cargo loading. When the second bell rang, indicating passenger boarding could commence, Pan Am expat families stood ready at the tender boat. The mood was tense, but under the direction of my cool-headed father, everyone remained calm and cooperative.

At that point, only Captain Ford and his crew knew the aircraft would be returning to New York via a hazardous westbound route, going the "wrong way" around the world.

Even though Flight Steward Verne Edwards would be on board, Daddy explained that no meal provisioning or in-flight service would be provided. With the exception of seats for us, the normally luxurious passenger cabins were now crammed with extra engine parts and other equipment supplies, all of which had been loaded in Auckland for *Pacific Clipper's* continued wartime journey.

As the last passengers to board, it seemed forever before Daddy said it was our turn. Dressed like a ridiculous doll in my sweltering wool suit, white gloves, and hat, I climbed onto the tender, but just as I was about to step through the entry door of the Clipper, a gust of wind caught my hat, blowing it into the water below. Keenly aware of Pan Am's strict dress code for employee travel, and remembering my mother's words, I panicked. Suddenly a world war was far less important than the fate of my hat. On the verge of tears, I froze, staring down at it bobbing on the water. Then, without an utterance or a tear from me--out of nowhere--a miracle happened. A muscular kanak, clad in a starched-white Pan Am uniform, dove in and rescued it!

Amid the confusion and drama of that hurried evacuation, it didn't occur to me or my parents to ask his name, but all these decades later, it was he—that kind man—who understood the importance of a little girl's hat. It is he who remains most vividly imbedded in the memory of a five-year-old girl.

Other memories of heroism live in my distant memory: the courage of Captain Ford and his crew; the unquestioning dedication of ground crews at every Pan Am station around the world; the local-hire Caledonians who were left to face whatever fate came their way, and, of course, my dear brother and remarkable parents.

Thanks to a voice recording my father made, I now know that the ground crew who were not airlifted that day lined up to bid farewell to *Pacific Clipper* as she taxied into the channel for takeoff. Standing at attention in their Pan Am "whites," they watched in silent tribute to *Pacific Clipper* as she departed from Noumea for the last time.

It wasn't until I was much older that I understood and appreciated that they and my family had become a small, but important part of Pan American's grand legend.

Epilogue

None of the evacuating passengers on board *Pacific Clipper* knew we were being flown to Gladstone, Australia, until after we were airborne from Noumea. Thereafter, Pan Am directed my family to make our own way from Gladstone to Sydney. First we took a train to Brisbane and, a few days later, another train to Sydney, where we spent Christmas and New Year. Eventually, my father received Pan Am instructions for us to board the USS *President Grant*. Once an American President Lines passenger ship, it had been taken over for the wartime transport of military personnel and supplies, plus occasional civilian evacuees like us.

While *Pacific Clipper* continued her epic journey around the world, my family and I remained completely in the dark about our own destiny. As it unfolded, we set sail from Sydney Harbor, often in zigzag defensive maneuvers, until arriving at Wellington, New Zealand, several days later. The rest of our highly secretive six weeks at sea took us to Peru and up the west coast of South and Central America until we docked at San Pedro, California. There my mother's family, who lived in Los Angeles, came to pick us up. For more than a month, they'd had no idea where we were, or if we were dead or alive.

Later, my father was sent to Miami to coordinate Pan Am's Air Ferries to Africa. We lived in Miami for the rest of WWII, followed by twenty-two years in South American countries.

Thanks to my intrepid family and Pan American, I've been blessed with a fascinating life!

Flying Boat Memoirs
Robert B. Hicks

CHAPTER 8

*M*y flying career began on Christmas Day, at age ten, during the Great Depression. After spending the day with my grandparents, my family was returning home when we saw an airplane parked in a pasture near Erick, Oklahoma, with a sign, "Ride 50 cents." On an impulse, I asked to spend the half dollar I had received in my Christmas stocking. My parents finally agreed, and I handed over my last penny for an airplane ride instead of candy bars. Then came the thrill of the takeoff and five whole minutes of flight.

In my second year of college, the federal government began a program to train flight instructors for the Army Air Corps. At the minimum age of nineteen, I immediately applied. After receiving my private pilot's license in August 1941, I began aerobatic training. Following the Pearl Harbor attack, I applied for navy pilot training, but failed the physical exam because of the missing first joint of my

US Navy PB2Y Coronado on the step. *Courtesy of PAHF.*

right index finger. Nevertheless, I went on to receive a commercial pilot license and flight instructor rating at Phoenix, Arizona, in July 1942. I then joined three classmates (Bill Farwell, Bob Berg, and Kit Smith) to fly for Pan American Airways in the Pacific Division with a starting junior pilot salary of $200 per month.

After I passed the medical exams and a probing psychological interview at Treasure Island, Pan Am Chief Pilot Joe "Red" Barrows welcomed me as a junior pilot with seniority No. 541. At about this time, the Pacific-Alaska Division became a part of Naval Air Transport Service (NATS). A dozen or more Navy flying boats, the PBM-3, and the PB2Y-3, were added to Pan Am's fleet of two Martin M-130s and six Boeing B-314 Clippers. All flight crews were inducted into the Naval Reserve on inactive duty. Captains were commissioned as lieutenant commanders, and I became an ensign.

Over the next couple of years, we studied seamanship, Morse code, semaphore (visual hand or flag signals), celestial navigation, meteorology, etiquette, and international aviation law. Flying boat training began in October on the twin-engine Martin Mariner (PBM-3). The instructor on my first training flight was Assistant Chief Pilot Bill Cluthe. He was an ex-navy pilot and one of Pan Am's most senior captains who had made several inaugural flights to the Orient and the South Pacific in the 1930s when he commanded the Sikorsky and Martin Clippers.

Along with four other junior pilots, I practiced takeoffs, landings, air work, and taxiing up to a buoy. I soon discovered that all maneuvers on water required multiple, simultaneous skills. Taxiing in San Francisco Bay on a windy day with tides and winds coming from opposite directions was tricky, particularly on the Martin and Boeing Clippers, which had sea wings instead of the pontoons common to Navy planes. Taxiing downwind from Treasure Island toward Berkeley, after making the 180-degree turn for takeoff into the wind, power had to be added only to the downwind engines to avoid dragging a wingtip in the water. Slowing the plane when approaching a buoy or dock required "blimping" the engines—continually pulling the master switch off and on to reduce the idling speed from 800 to 200 rpm—all the while keeping an eye on the gauges and a sharp lookout for boats or debris floating in the bay. To secure the aircraft to mooring docks, the bowman (usually a junior crewmember) had to catch the heavy bowline floating in the water with a grapnel, and place the loop over the bow post. This was a unique skill requiring physical strength and quick action.

Takeoffs were exhilarating on the flying boats, especially in rough water on a windy day. Water pounded on the hull like hail on a tin roof until we could gain enough speed to skim the surface. This was challenging at full gross weight, especially at Pearl Harbor with little wind and smooth water. Getting onto the "step" (a structural feature designed to reduce drag on the hull) and to break suction on the hull required rocking the yoke backward and forward.

In November 1942, I qualified as third pilot on all of Pan Am's flying boats. My first scheduled flight was from San Francisco to Honolulu on December 22, 1942, with Capt. Fred Richards. The M-130 *Philippine Clipper* crew of eleven met for a one-hour safety drill before we marched two abreast to board the airplane at the dock. After leveling out at cruising altitude (usually 7,000 to 9,000 feet depending on the wind), the first officer would prepare the "watch list," assigning duty time for each crewmember. He was also responsible for relieving the navigator for a couple of hours during the night.

Droning along at 115 knots (135 mph) in clear weather with a navigator (the second officer), a radio operator, and a flight engineer at their stations, there was little to do, particularly when the plane was on autopilot. With no weather stations and no en route radio aids, crossing vast areas of land and sea depended entirely on the

Philippine Clipper on shake-down flight over California coast. Courtesy of PAHF.

crew's knowledge and application of celestial or dead reckoning navigation, which was limited to observing our drift when the ocean below was not obscured.

During that seventeen-hour-and-thirty-minute flight to Pearl Harbor, I logged four hours and twenty minutes at the controls. After a two-day layover at the Moana Hotel, I returned to Treasure Island on the world-renowned *China Clipper.* As a reminder that it was wartime, we had to circle the offshore Farallon Islands before approaching San Francisco Bay to avoid being shot down as enemy aircraft.

On February 2, 1943, I would have been lost at sea on the *China Clipper* in a severe winter storm if the captain had not made a wise decision. The eleven-man crew consisted of Capt. R. J. Nixon, First Officer (and relief navigator) Mathew "Rip" Van Winkle, the second officer (navigator), myself as third officer, two flight engineers, two radiomen, and two stewards. We departed Pearl Harbor shortly after noon and climbed to our cruising altitude. At this point, Capt. Nixon removed his uniform and retired to a bunk, leaving the first and third officers to do all the en route flying. As was often his custom, Capt. Nixon would return to the cockpit to make the landing.

The problem began about nine hours after takeoff. Soon after midnight, the sky was becoming obscured by an unusually strong winter storm moving rapidly into the Northern California coastal area, greatly hindering attempts at celestial navigation. As we approached the forecasted equal time point (ETP, the critical point of no return when it's a shorter time to continue than to turn back), the navigator/second officer informed Van Winkle that our speed had decreased from 135 mph to 70 mph. The first engineer, obviously concerned, told Van Winkle that at a speed of 70 mph, our fuel would be exhausted 450 miles short of San Francisco. Van Winkle was sure we were in no danger as he was able to take a star fix. It confirmed our speed. However, we would soon have a 300-degree quartering tailwind when we turned right for the final 1,000 miles to San Francisco. Unfortunately, he was relying on erroneous Morse code progress reports sent hourly from a westbound Pan Am B-314. Unintentionally, they had transposed an important two-digit number—a small but potentially fatal mistake. Also, the actual speed of the westbound B-314 was not transmitted because the obscured sky prevented star fixes.

As the flight progressed, the flight engineer began demanding that Van Winkle inform the captain. Still convinced we were in no danger, Van Winkle ignored him. He was positive that once past the forecasted ETP, and thereby committed to continue, we would avoid the cost of a turnaround and the inconvenience to passengers. At nearly thirteen and a half hours out of Honolulu, now with the frantic engineer shouting that he was going to call the captain out of his bunk, Van Winkle finally agreed.

Capt. Nixon appeared in his white skivvies and leaned on the navigation table to review the chart. Van Winkle explained his decision to continue, and the engineer argued that by doing so, we would be landing in a wild storm hundreds of miles from San Francisco. After maybe only a minute, Nixon straightened up and said, "Turn back," and returned to his bunk.

The engineer set the power for long-range cruise, and the navigator stuck a note on the instrument panel with a compass heading for Hilo, which was closer than Honolulu. If we were going to make an ocean landing, it would be in calm, warm Hawaiian waters rather than in a raging ocean somewhere west of San Francisco.

As soon as the sky was clear enough, star fixes confirmed that a strong tailwind had been giving us a speed of over 200 mph for a few hours. Snow-capped Mauna Kea appeared a hundred miles dead ahead in a gray dawn. Knowing we had plenty of fuel, the navigator gave me a new heading of about thirty degrees to the right for Honolulu, and the stewards began preparing breakfast for our weary passengers.

After nineteen hours and forty minutes in the air, Capt.Nixon was notified of our approach and appeared in his uniform in time to make the landing at Pearl Harbor.

In silent thanks to Capt. Nixon and the insistent engineer, I celebrated my twenty-first birthday on the white sand shores of Waikiki Beach!

On June 11, 1943, I passed my check flight on the PBM with Capt. Beer, the most senior pilot in the Pacific-Alaska Division. Afterwards, I was assigned to live at the Moana Hotel in Waikiki for the next few months, flying the PBM as first officer on South Pacific flights. Overnights were at Palmyra, Canton, Funafuti, Suva, Noumea, Auckland, Brisbane, and Espiritu Santo. Landings for fuel, cargo, and passengers were also made at Wallis, a mountainous, jungle-covered island in French Samoa between Canton and Fiji. The week-long round trips required nearly seventy flight hours. Between flights, I kicked back at the Moana Hotel; surfboarding in the morning and playing afternoon volleyball at the Outrigger Club, and, after dinner, poker in the Moana's "Black Out" room until the ten o'clock curfew. On Saturday afternoons, from the courtyard under the hotel's spectacular banyan tree, I watched Harry Owens and his band perform the live broadcast *Hawaii Calls* with Hilo Hattie singing and dancing the hula.

In late 1943, I reported for an early morning departure from Suva, Fiji, to Auckland, New Zealand. Before noon, we arrived at the US Navy Base at Noumea, New Caledonia, for an overnight. The third officer and I decided to have lunch at the naval officers' club, which was next to a narrow channel separating the club from four ships tied up at a huge dock where hundreds of sailors were unloading ammunition.

Instead of dining at the club, we ended up munching on sandwiches on a low stone wall with our backs to the dock. Suddenly, there was a tremendous explosion behind us. My shirt puffed out as I was blown off the wall. My first thought was that the Japanese were attacking. On my hands and knees, I looked up to see debris blowing 300 feet high. Sailors dove into the water and swam across the narrow channel toward us as ammunition on the dock continued exploding for the next two hours. It took about three hours before the ships' officers could get enough crewmembers back to the ships to move them away from the dock. The disastrous Noumea explosions took the lives of 250 US Navy sailors.

The morning of February 10, 1944, I nearly met my demise as an extra pilot on the B-314 *California Clipper* during a flight between Treasure Island and Pearl Harbor. The third officer had cast off and secured the bow for departure, and I had volunteered to man the bow on arrival at Pearl Harbor. As the plane began descending near Molokai, I wanted to be certain all the arrival equipment I would need was easily on hand (bow post, hooks, machete, etc.), so I crawled between Captain Hale and First Officer "Doc" Anderson to the ladder and climbed down into the bow compartment where cargo and mailbags were stowed. At the forward portside of the bow was a six-foot-high cargo hatch in two sections, one above the other. The upper section opened only inward with the hinges on the forward side. The lower section only opened out and downward, like the tailgate of a pickup truck. As I went down the ladder, I noticed the bow compartment was unusually noisy, perhaps, I reasoned, because of the higher descent airspeed. Then I saw that two of the five "dogs," or latches, for the upper section of the cargo hatch were not secured. In the unpressurized airplanes of the day, outside pressure from the airstream was pushing the trailing edge inward about half an inch. Instead of reporting the problem to my crewmates, I decided to fix it myself. All I had to do was push the upper section of the hatch hard enough to be able to close the latches. What could be easier?

I stepped into a narrow space between the mailbags and the hatch, pushed hard, and got the shock of my life! Without warning, the upper inward opening section of the hatch blasted outward, snapping both metal hinges. Off it flew into the slipstream, just inside and below the number two prop, barely missing the horizontal stabilizer.

The lower cargo door was now unlatched, flopping violently from a gaping hole that extended from my feet to above my head. Off balance from pushing outward, and with the descent speed of 180 mph trying to suck me out, I was surely on my way to follow the lost hatch to the beckoning whitecaps 7,000 feet below. Desperately, I clung to the feeble cargo netting while the lower section oscillated wildly up and down amid the tornado-like roar of the engines. If plunging into the sea didn't end my life, the whirling engine propeller, only a few feet away, threatened to do a superb job.

Moments later, my predicament became even more dire when the plane entered turbulent cumulus clouds. Trying to keep my precarious footing, I didn't think things could get any worse. But they did.

My lifeline—the netting—was coming loose! In that horrifying moment, I had no choice but to relinquish my grip. Amid the roar of engines and wind rushing through the compartment's gaping hole, I reached for the metal ladder. With a white-knuckled grip, I pulled myself closer, able to get my arm completely around it. For what seemed hours, but was only a matter of seconds, I literally hung on for dear life until I was able to climb up to the cockpit.

Obviously unconcerned at my frazzled appearance, First Officer Anderson looked at me and casually said, "You look a little green. We were about to check on you."

I was speechless. A few moments later, the flight engineer reported that a Navy officer seated in the passenger cabin had seen an aircraft inspection plate "sail" past his window. Capt. Hale immediately radioed Pearl Harbor, declaring an emergency. Weak-kneed, I stood behind him as we set down at Pearl, where four rescue boats were stationed alongside the landing area.

The next day, I departed as first officer with Capt. Hale in a PBM-3 on a seven-day trip from Honolulu to New Zealand and back. On the return, dispatch informed me that instead of remaining in Honolulu at the fabulous Moana Hotel, I was being reassigned to Treasure Island. The *California Clipper* was, by then, back in service with a new hatch. Chief Pilot Joe Barrows called me into his office. Refusing to hear my side of the story, he ordered me to work forty hours in the shop—the man-hours required to rivet sheet metal in place for a hatch.

Pan Am had a well-staffed meteorology department, and as crewmembers, we spent many hours in classes taught by Chief Meteorologist Serebreny, but in those early days of aviation, little was known about the weather. It was not until after the era of the flying boats that meteorology further developed, and pilots began learning about jet streams, wind shear, and microbursts—and how dangerous thunderstorms could be.

My worst encounter with a thunderstorm occurred on May 31, 1944, in a PBM on return from Espiritu Santo to Honolulu with Capt. Bart Randolph, who had flown into many thunderstorms in the Latin American Division. Near the equator, there was always a band of towering, mushrooming cumulonimbus clouds, sometimes 50,000 feet high, called the "stationary equatorial front." In spite of the threats thunderstorms presented, if pilots couldn't fly around them, they could usually find a "light," or safe, spot to enter and exit.

On this day, however, there were no light spots. Approaching at 8,500 feet, we faced a very dark wall of clouds as far as we could see on both sides of the aircraft. Unable to see any light spots, Capt. Randolph headed straight into the front. To reduce stress on the airframe, he reduced the power and airspeed, but when the plane became uncontrollable due to heavy turbulence, Randolph turned back.

Once back in clear air, we flew a few minutes to the right, then went directly back into the violent storm. Once again Randolph turned around, flying several minutes to the left before heading back into the front, but the turbulence was so violent, he was again forced to return to clear air.

At that point, Capt. Randolph breathtakingly spiraled the aircraft down to 500 feet, and retackled the storm. We ran into an unexpected, massive wall of swirling water. With the air speed dropping fifteen knots, the altimeter down to a dangerous 350 feet, and the vertical speed indicator showing a descent of 300 to 400 feet per minute, Randolph shouted for full power. Pushing the fuel mixture, the prop controls, and throttles to full forward, after a few tense moments, we began to hold and then gain altitude and air speed. Then, suddenly, miraculously, we popped out of the storm into a clear blue sky, all in one piece.

We were trained not to attempt guessing our height above the water on night landings, particularly in unlit South Pacific lagoons where there were no runway lights and the water was usually smooth, without whitecaps, and deceptive to the eye. On one arrival at Canton Atoll in a PBM at about ten o'clock on a dark, moonless night, Capt. Randolph gave me the landing. Keeping my eye on the altimeter, using one hand, I made the final approach, maintaining a descent of 200 feet per minute by adjusting the throttles to control the rate of descent and the airspeed. With my other hand on the yoke, I kept the nose high and the wings perfectly level. To avoid overrunning the landing area, the approach needed to clear the lighted buildings and docks in our path, but at the same time, we had to be low enough to make contact with the water within seconds without stalling the plane. Capt. Randolph watched silently as I aimed toward a small, lighted boat half a mile ahead. We hit the water with a jolt, and I immediately chopped the power and pulled back the yoke as far as possible to keep the bow from being sucked down into the water. The landing was perfect, but Capt. Randolph never said a word.

My last year and a half on the flying boats was not as eventful as the first year and a half. I flew most flights as first officer on the Navy Coronado (the Consolidated PB2Y-3). It was a seaplane version of the B-24 Air Force bomber, primarily a cargo plane but with up to twenty additional passenger seats. It had none of the luxuries of the B-314 Clippers.

Although I had enough seniority to fly as a first officer on the more glamorous B-314s, I did not mind longer assignments to the South Pacific on other aircraft. I especially didn't mind three weeks off between scheduled trips.

Even though I never reached the rank of captain, I flew as one on some occasions. In late afternoon of February 5, 1945, I arrived at the San Francisco Airport for a cargo flight to Honolulu on the PB2Y. Capt. Ralph Richey was waiting for me in the dimly lit hallway of the operations office wearing dark sunglasses and the appearance of a bad sunburn. Taking me by the arm, he told me in low tones that I would have to handle the flight. While working on the engine of his 1909 Stanley Steamer car, there had been an explosion that had temporarily impaired his eyesight and singed his eyebrows and eyelashes.

After helping him sign necessary paperwork, we boarded the aircraft for departure. Soon after dark, with Capt. Richey in the left seat still wearing his sunglasses, I made the takeoff. The weather was fair, and the overnight flight to Honolulu was uneventful with the third officer and me doing all the flying. After a three-day layover in Honolulu, Capt. Richey no longer needed his sunglasses and was able to resume his captain duties.

In April 1945, flying the *Honolulu Clipper* to Honolulu and the *Dixie Clipper* back to San Francisco with Capt. Jack Myers, I completed the required 200 hours of navigation time on scheduled flights and was licensed a celestial navigator. Having reached the minimum age of twenty-three, and having logged the required 1,200 hours of pilot time, I began training for my airline transport pilot license. I received it on June 4, 1945, after a tough one-hour check ride by Civil Aeronautics Inspector John Burns.

In early June 1945, at least twenty of the most senior first officers in the Pacific Division, including me, were notified that we were being transferred to Miami to check out as captains on the DC-3s. We were to fly soldiers returning from overseas to destinations within the States. Training in the Pre-Command School in Miami was to begin in only two short months.

For personal and professional reasons, I chose to remain in the Pacific Division, but before turning down Miami, I asked Chief Pilot "Brick" Maxwell if I could remain at Treasure Island as a first officer. I offered a "deal" of lower seniority until the B-314s would be phased out. His answer was, "Take the transfer or be terminated."

Pan Am's flying boats were the most glamorous passenger airplanes ever flown, reaching the most exciting and exotic places around the world. I was proud and privileged to have been part of the company's final flying boat era in the Pacific. Exchanging that legacy for a DC-3 pilot position in Miami was not a compromise I was willing to make.

My flying boat career lasted only three years, but was certainly the most memorable period in my life. Flying the Martin M-130 *China* and *Philippine* Clippers and the Boeing B-314 *Honolulu*, *California*, *Atlantic*, and *Dixie* Clippers from Treasure Island to Pearl Harbor, as well as the navy airplanes throughout the South Pacific, was an experience never to be forgotten. Never to be repeated.

I logged more than 6,000 pilot and navigation hours, and during seventy-three years as an active pilot, I had no accidents, forced landings, failed check rides, or citations. For this, I owe much to the $70,000-worth of Pan Am training. Also, to Pan Am's credit, I was able to study at Stanford University while on a medical leave. Eventually I received a BS degree in engineering and an MBA, which later afforded me a business career.

Resigning from Pan Am was a tough decision, one I regretted at times. But the great flying boats were gone. Pan Am was entering a new phase of political complications and increasing competition from other airlines. For me, it just wasn't the same airline that had hired me in 1942.

Pan American opened many doors for me, including lucrative work with the Disney Corporation. But more than anything else, I'm grateful for the Honolulu trips, from which I brought home fresh

PAA Douglas DC-3 Airliner. Courtesy of PAHF.

Bob Hicks at the 2016 Irish Spring Reunion, Foynes, Ireland. Courtesy of Teresa Webber.

flower lei two or three times a month. Those fragrant garlands (and perhaps my Waikiki suntan) helped eliminate the competition for Gerry, my wife of seventy-one years.

Most certainly, the best money I ever spent was for a five-minute, fifty-cent plane ride.

Pan Am at War

Robert Gand

CHAPTER 9

Sunday morning, 7 December 1941

An era was ending. In the space of a few violent hours, the United States had shed its lofty detachment from the conflicts of Europe and Asia. And as the dawn rolled westward over the Pacific, the most glamorous chapter in commercial aviation was coming to a close. The transpacific routes pioneered by Pan American Airways— and the elegant chain of specially constructed island bases—were now a combat zone.

Philippine Clipper approaching Wake Lagoon Pier. Courtesy of PAHF.

America was at war, and so was Pan Am.

One of the first to know was Lanier Turner, captain of Pan American's B-314 flying boat *Anzac Clipper*. Turner and his crew of ten, with their seventeen passengers, were an hour from arrival at Pearl Harbor when they received the report: Pearl Harbor was under attack by enemy airplanes. Stunned, Turner pulled out the ship's briefcase that contained his sealed war emergency orders.

Farther to the west, the Martin M-130 *Philippine Clipper*, commanded by Capt. John "Hammy" Hamilton, had just taken off from Wake Island lagoon, bound for Guam. By radio Hamilton received the news about the Japanese attack on Hawaii. And with the news came new orders: The *Philippine Clipper* was to return immediately to Wake and evacuate all Pan American personnel. An enemy attack on the island could come at any time.

In the South Pacific, the B-314 flying boat *Pacific Clipper* was midway between New Caledonia and New Zealand, en route to Auckland. Capt. Bob Ford learned about the Japanese attack with the further news that the Japanese were on the move throughout the Far East. It meant that the *Pacific Clipper's* return route to the US had been cut off.

Standing on the seaplane dock at Hong Kong Kai Tak airport, Capt. Fred Ralph was watching the ground crew finish loading the *Hong Kong Clipper*, a Pan American S-42B flying boat. Ralph had already been briefed about the Pearl Harbor attack, and his orders now were to get the Clipper—and its passengers—out of Hong Kong before the Japanese arrived. His scheduled destination, Manila, was already under attack. Ralph's plan was to fly the S-42B to Kunming, China, landing in a nearby lake.

In the next instant, Ralph realized they were too late. He heard the rumble of engines. To the north, he spotted the silhouettes of airplanes descending over Sha Tin Pass. They were headed directly for Kai Tak.

On the opposite side of the planet, Pan American president Juan Trippe was at his rolltop desk in the Pan American offices of the Chrysler Building. It was Sunday afternoon in New York. Trippe was trying to make sense of the incoming reports. All Pan American's ocean bases—Honolulu, Midway, Wake, Guam, Manila, Hong Kong—were in jeopardy. In even greater jeopardy were four of his precious flying boats. Their crews and passengers were out there somewhere, caught up in the Pacific war.

Aboard the *Anzac Clipper*, still inbound to Pearl Harbor, Capt. Lanier Turner opened the sealed contingency orders that flew aboard every transpacific Pan American flight. The instructions seemed clear enough: Turner was supposed to divert his flight to Hilo, on the island of Hawaii, about 150 miles south of Pearl Harbor. But

Turner had cause to be worried. The instructions had been written before anyone knew *where*—or from what direction—an enemy might attack. Where was the Japanese task force now? Was an invasion coming? Were enemy fighters in the air between him and Hilo? Would Hilo also come under attack?

No one knew. Not until two hours later, when he alighted in the harbor at Hilo, did Turner learn the extent of the destruction at Pearl Harbor. He intended to refuel and immediately depart for San Francisco, but he found that there was no Pan American staff at Hilo, nor were there pressure fuel pumps. Fueling the giant flying boat by hand took the crew until the next day. On the night of Monday, December 8, they departed Hilo in blackness and radio silence. By the time *Anzac Clipper* reached California, Turner and his crew had neither shaved nor slept in a bed for seventy-two hours.

At Wake Island, beyond the International Date Line, John Hamilton had just landed the *Philippine Clipper* back in the lagoon when the Navy and Marine commanders of the Wake garrison presented him with a request: Before he took off and headed east, would he take the *Philippine Clipper* on a patrol, escorted by Marine fighters, to sweep the sea around Wake for incoming enemy forces?

Hamilton agreed. But while the big Clipper was still being fueled at her mooring, Hamilton heard the distant drone of engines. Flying beneath a low squall line, two formations of enemy aircraft came roaring in from the north.

In the next few minutes, the Pan American base, built with the spirit and sweat of adventurers from the expedition ship *North Haven*, was blown to bits. The Clipper loading dock disappeared in a geyser of debris. A Japanese warplane strafed the *Philippine Clipper*, stitching a line of bullets across the fuselage.

When the enemy planes had left, Hamilton climbed from the ditch where he'd taken cover. Smoke was billowing from the destroyed facilities. He ran to the Martin flying boat, expecting the worst. Despite the bullet holes in her fuselage, the *Philippine Clipper* appeared to be intact. Hamilton gave the order to strip every nonessential item from the aircraft—cargo, baggage, passenger amenities—and round up all the passengers and Pan American employees.

With thirty-four people on board, including two seriously wounded, Hamilton taxied the flying boat into the lagoon. On the first takeoff attempt, the overloaded Clipper refused to lift from the water. Hamilton tried again—with the same result. On the third attempt, Hamilton finally coaxed the *Philippine Clipper's* hull off the water. Laboring into the air, skimming low over the sandy beach, the flying boat headed eastward.

It was a bittersweet moment. Left to face the enemy were the Marines defending Wake, as well as the civilian construction workers who had come to build the fighter strip. Nor was the *Philippine Clipper* out of harm's way. Japanese warplanes owned the sky and most of the sea.

Droning through the darkness, Hamilton learned that Midway, too, had come under attack. From miles away, he could see the fires that stood out like a beacon in the night. Hamilton picked out a landing path on the debris-strewn lagoon and managed to bring the Clipper down safely. The next day, he and his fellow escapees from Wake flew to Pearl Harbor, then homeward to San Francisco.

In the British Crown Colony of Hong Kong, air raid sirens were wailing. Fred Ralph and his crew saw the first bombs rain down on Kai Tak airport. Sprinting for cover, they jumped into the water behind concrete dock pilings, realizing too late that they'd chosen an open sewer for shelter.

Explosions rocked the colony. From his shelter, Ralph watched Japanese Zero fighters diving on the moored *Hong Kong Clipper*. Ralph had a special affection for the old Sikorsky flying boat. Her nickname was *Myrtle*, and she'd been brought to the Far East to service the Manila-Hong Kong segment of the transpacific air route.

Ralph counted six passes. On each pass the enemy bullets traced a path across the dock and into the water—missing the Clipper. On the seventh pass, the incendiary bullets struck home. Ralph watched helplessly as Myrtle erupted in flames and burned to the waterline.

That night Ralph and his crew escaped Hong Kong aboard a CNAC (Chinese affiliate of Pan Am) DC-2. For a month, like wandering refugees, they meandered across Asia and Europe, not reaching New York until January 1942. It was then they learned that Hong Kong had fallen to the Japanese on Christmas Day.

Meanwhile in Auckland, New Zealand, Bob Ford, captain of the *Pacific Clipper*, was considering his options. The Pacific had become a battleground. The route to the US via Pan American's island bases had been severed by the Japanese. Ford and his crew reached a decision: They would take "the long way home."

And they did. In an epic journey that became the stuff of legend, the *Pacific Clipper* flew westward across the Indian Ocean, the Middle East, the Arabian peninsula, the continent of Africa, across the South Atlantic, and up the coasts of South and North America. Avoiding enemy planes and ships, bartering for fuel, parts, and food, the Clipper and her crew overflew three oceans and alighted and took off from harbors and rivers in twelve different countries.

On the morning of January 6, 1942, the startled duty officer in New York heard the radio transmission: "*Pacific Clipper* inbound from Auckland, New Zealand. Due arrive Pan American Marine Terminal LaGuardia seven minutes."

They had entered history. The *Pacific Clipper's* 31,500-mile odyssey was the longest yet made by a commercial aircraft and the first around the world.

Pan American was now at war, but the truth was that the airline had *already* mobilized for war. More than a year earlier, Juan Trippe had executed a contract with the War Department for the construction of airfields and facilities across South America and Africa. He also made a deal to transfer three advanced B-314 flying boats to BOAC, flag airline of embattled Britain. Two new divisions—Pan American Airways-Africa and Pan American Air Ferries—had been created to operate an aerial highway from the US to the Middle East.

Pan American's ocean bases at Wake, Guam, Manila, and Hong Kong all fell to the Japanese. Thirty-eight Pan Am employees became prisoners of the Japanese. Pan Am's Chinese affiliate, CNAC, managed to evacuate nearly 400 adults and children from besieged Hong Kong before the colony surrendered.

The age of elegance was officially over. Pan American's fleet of luxurious flying boats—nine Boeing B-314s and two Martin M-130 flying boats, including the famous *China Clipper*—were converted to military transports. Every amenity—seats, berths, lounges—were ripped from the aircraft. Each took on a coat of dull sea-gray paint.

By the end of the war three and a half years later, the world had irrevocably changed—and so had Pan American. Pan Am had flown over ninety million miles in wartime service, more than double the total of all other US airlines. Pan Am crews made more than 18,000 ocean crossings and ferried more than 500 military aircraft to combat zones. The airline trained more than 5,000 pilots, navigators, and mechanics for wartime duty. Pan Am oversaw the construction of

more than fifty airports around the planet. For his airline's contributions to the war effort, Trippe was presented with the Medal for Merit— the highest civilian decoration of the United States.

And nothing more. Trippe's bright expectations of post-war recognition and reward for Pan American were not realized. The entry of the US domestic airlines in the military transport effort had broken Pan Am's exclusivity on overseas routes. Now the US airlines were clamoring for authority on the same routes that Pan American had pioneered in the pre-war years. In the coming era, Pan American would compete not only with the airlines of foreign countries but also with the domestic carriers of the US.

For Pan Am, the war was over, but another was just beginning.

The Art Deco Era
of Pan Am Terminals
James Trautman

CHAPTER 10

*"Like the great railway stations, airports are also the contemporary
equivalents of gateways. Very often, they represent your first experience of
a city or country. In that sense they have the potential to excite and inspire."*

Pan Am founder Juan Trippe insisted that traveling on board
his Clippers would be singular experiences; likewise, that
exquisite Pan Am terminal buildings would create unforgettable
memories of his company. He spared no expense on either.

During the age of the great flying boats, and prior to WWII,
Pan American built three magnificent gateway buildings on the US
mainland. In 1934, the first was opened at Dinner Key in Miami's
Coral Gables. The second was located at Treasure Island in San
Francisco Bay, completed in 1939. The third was the Marine Air
Terminal (MAT) in New York, which opened in 1940, at North
Beach Field, the present site of LaGuardia Airport. All three were
representative of the classic elegance of the art deco period. Today,
each exists in one form or another, but only the LaGuardia terminal
remains functional in its originally intended use for air transportation.

From the ground up, Pan Am built landing sites, hotels, and
terminals on the Pacific "stepping stone" atolls of Wake and Midway.
Although these terminals were far less grand in size, style, and design
than their US mainland art deco counterparts, they were equally
important for the company's image and the comfort of passengers
(see chapter 3).

Dinner Key

Dinner Key is a small island in Biscayne Bay. It was joined to the
Florida mainland during WWI to provide a training field for the US
Navy. Used by non-scheduled commercial airlines until after the war,
it was destroyed during the September 1926 hurricane—commonly
known as the "Great Miami Hurricane," or the "Big Blow."

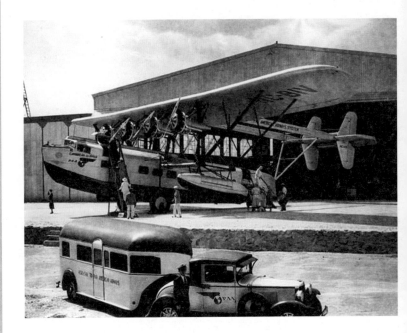

In 1930, the newly formed Pan American Airways secured rights from the US government to fly commercial mail and passengers from New York City to Buenos Aires. The unusually swift approval caught Trippe off guard. It required the immediate need for a transiting terminus in Miami. With no time to construct an elaborate terminal, the temporary solution was a houseboat, purchased by Pan Am in Havana. Immediately towed to Dinner Key, it was anchored to pilings and barges. Passengers transferring from domestic airlines or from ground transportation were delivered to the makeshift terminal aboard a unique car-trailer contraption, clearly marked with Pan Am's logo.

A year later, in 1931, Miami's mayor, H. C. Reeder, broke ground for a permanent building. Plans for the new Dinner Key facility would accommodate up to thirty-five aircraft daily and would include runways for land aircraft, but runways were soon abandoned for two reasons: There was no way to lengthen them for heavier, larger aircraft, and more importantly, Pan Am was focused entirely on its flying boats (the twin engine Commodores and the new Sikorsky S-40s).

In order to accommodate the deeper hulls of the S-40s, airport engineers dredged the surrounding shallow waters to a depth of six feet. This became the standard depth for all future flying boats contracts.

Dinner Key's rectangular, two-story terminal was designed by the acclaimed architectural firm Delano & Aldrich. It included one-story wings on each side, white stucco exterior walls, and a flat roof. Extending around the building, just below the cornice, was a frieze of winged globes and rising suns, connected at the corners by sculptured eagles, all exquisitely representing the art deco style of the day.

To the thrill of passengers and their guests, Clipper operations were observed from the upper-level restaurant and bar of Dinner Key. From a nearby road, spectators parked their automobiles and watched spellbound as the amazing flying machines took off and set down.

Situated inside the first-floor level were comfortable passenger waiting rooms, plus the conveniences of an International Mail Office, US Customs, Immigration, Public Health offices, and ticket counters. Art deco murals depicted the history of aviation; panels with elaborate zodiac signs loomed above in the coffered ceiling, and a giant silver-painted winged clock displayed local time.

Dinner Key terminal building showing observation deck. *Courtesy of PAHF.*

The star attraction of the Dinner Key Marine Terminal was a massive, three-and-a-half-ton world globe. Ten feet in diameter with a thirty-one-and-a-half-foot circumference, it was accurate to a scale of one inch to sixty-four nautical miles and was aligned to the Earth's axis at the Miami location. To the awe of thousands of visitors, an electric motor rotated it every two minutes, allowing everyone to easily locate all of Pan Am's worldwide destinations. The globe now resides in the entrance hall of the Miami Museum of Science and Technology.

In 1952, six years after the flying boats became obsolete, Pan Am sold Dinner Key to the City of Miami for one million dollars. The structure later became the Miami City Hall, where a plaque now describes the building's historical significance, and where much of the original grandeur has been maintained or restored.

Treasure Island

With Dinner Key in place, Trippe turned his attention to the West Coast of the United States, where Pan Am needed to establish terminals and outlying bases for its Pacific routes. Already in existence was the Alameda Airport and control tower, from which the famous *China Clipper* departed in 1935 on its epic journey to Manila (see chapter 4).

The success of Chicago's 1933 "Century of Progress World's Fair"—also known as the "Aviation World's Fair," at which flying boats were highlighted—inspired Pan Am and the city of San Francisco to seek approval for an international exposition. The public was fascinated with anything connected to aviation. San

Francisco and Pan Am hoped to use this to their advantage. They reasoned that an event on the scale of previous world fairs would help finance a new terminal facility. However, the Roosevelt administration denied the request, on the grounds that Public Works money could be used only for highways and airports. The original proposal had not mentioned either.

Realizing their error, the city and Pan American submitted a new proposal, and this one included an airport. Pan Am would relocate its Alameda operation from across the bay to Treasure Island.

The only catch in the plan was that the island didn't yet exist. And so, in 1936–37, the federal government built an artificial island using dredged sediment from the bay and imported fill. Named

Art Deco Terminals

The term art deco comes from the 1925 Paris Exposition *Internationale des Arts Decoratifs Industriels et Modernes*. It is a diversified style, combining traditional repeated craft designs with Machine Age imagery and materials. Adopted by architects and designers of jewelry, furniture, and fashion from around the world, it was the most popular style of modern art from 1925 until the mid-1940s, when it lost popularity during the Great Depression and WWII.

Art deco is characterized by deep, rich colors, lavish ornamentation, symmetry, and bold geometric shapes with added curved ornamental elements. Materials include stucco, concrete, smooth-faced stone, and terra-cotta. Steel and aluminum were often used along with glass blocks, as was decorative opaque plate glass. Architects adorned flat roofs with parapets, spires, or towers, which were also used to accentuate a corner or entrance.

During its height of popularity, art deco represented luxury, glamour, and the public's belief in social and technological progress.

In addition to Pan Am's exemplary art deco terminals, other fine examples are the Chrysler Building in New York City and the world-famous Christ the Redeemer statue looming above Rio de Janeiro.

Le salon de Paul Reynaud, by Jean-Pierre Dalbéra, Paris, France. *Public domain.*

Chrysler Building lobby, NYC. Site of the early Pan American Airways offices. *Public domain.*

after the novel *Treasure Island* by Robert Louis Stevenson, who lived in San Francisco from 1879 to 1880, the new island was connected by a small isthmus to the north side of Yerba Buena Island between San Francisco and Oakland.

After the Public Works Commission approved the Golden Gate International Exposition, the United States would have two fairs in 1939 and 1940, one in San Francisco, the other in New York. Both fairs would feature Pan American's show-stopping flying boats.

In August 1938, Pan American signed a twenty-year lease for the Treasure Island facility. Meanwhile, architect George W. Kelham had been commissioned to design the exposition's administration building, which would later become the airport's terminal. The first of two structures to be built was a hangar with a ramp railway that moved the Clippers to and from the water.

To entice the public's interest in the upcoming exposition, as well as publicize the relocation of Pan American, teams of pretty young ladies dressed in pirate costumes handed out thousands of advertising flyers: "Every once in a while, somewhere on earth there occurs an event so extraordinary that it enriches forever the lives of all who witness it. San Francisco in 1939 promises just such an experience."

It was a big bill to fill, but when the exposition opened on Saturday morning, February 18, 1939, it delivered. The Golden Gate International Exposition was an enormous success, and Pan American drew wide-eyed visitors by the droves.

The exposition's taxi, mooring area, and hangars were located next to a lagoon, which was soon dubbed "Clipper Cove." It quickly became a popular gathering place where spectators and picnickers could watch the Clippers coming and going. Every exposition map prominently featured Pan Am's stunning Art Deco terminal, Clipper Cove, and images of the world-famous flying Clippers.

Pan Am built three permanent structures on Treasure Island. The main one served as the administration building during the exposition and eventually served as the terminal's extravagant art deco entrance and control tower. Located in the building's wings were a weather station, public observation galleries, restaurants, and offices. In the basement were designated areas for mail delivery, freight, and customer services. Outside were five loading ramps for the flying boats.

Similar to Dinner Key, the main Treasure Island building was adorned in art deco style, featuring blue-colored stone carvings of King Neptune holding the Pan Am *China Clipper* and gigantic concrete figures guarding the entrance doors. The interior walls were painted in aviation motifs, now sadly painted over in a military theme. Also as at Dinner Key, an enormous world globe took center stage. It is now on display at the Lou Turpin Aviation Museum at the San Francisco International Airport.

Long after the exposition ended, thousands flocked daily to Treasure Island, thrilled to see the Clippers take off and land. They marveled at the sharply uniformed crews marching to and from the terminal, ever hopeful to catch sight of famous passengers who frequented the flying boats. Treasure Island was not only functional, it was a tremendous advertising and public relations tool for Pan American.

When Japan attacked Pearl Harbor in 1941, the US Navy took control of Treasure Island, making it a central part of the military structure throughout the war. Under military control, Pan Am's flying boats, flight crews, and ground staff remained operational.

Wake and Midway

The Pacific "stepping stone" atolls of Wake and Midway, with nothing more than a skeleton crew operating a cable station, served as overnight stops for passengers and crews between Honolulu and Guam. Honolulu was a well-established tourist destination where Pan Am provided first-class hotel accommodations on the halcyon

Pan Am "Airway Inn" Hotel, Wake Island. *Courtesy of PAHF.*

shores of Waikiki Beach. Though not measuring up to the luxurious amenities of Honolulu's Moana or Royal Hawaiian hotels, accommodations at Wake and Midway were something of a wonder.

Both hotels, each with forty-five guest rooms, arrived as prefabricated buildings on board the SS *North Haven* between 1935 and 1936. Designed by Delano & Aldrich, they were quickly erected to be ready for the inbound flying boats. The island-style hotels included separate rooms for each passenger, a full dining room serving high-quality meals, and enough recreational opportunities to keep passengers busy during their brief layovers.

After long flights from either Honolulu or Guam, most passengers preferred to simply relax on the lanai, lounging in wicker chairs, while sipping cocktails and exchanging travel tales. More energetic souls could stroll the powdery white sand beaches, swim in the tepid warm sea, or try their hand at "Goony Golf," a makeshift sport invented by the "stranded" crews of the *North Haven*.

Both of Pan Am's blissful island bases were destroyed early in WWII during Japanese invasions. The infamously bloody Battle of Wake, with high casualties on both sides, was fought from December 7 to 23, 1941. Many of Pan American's personnel fought valiantly alongside US Marines (see chapter 9).

Marine Air Terminal, New York

Now with completed Pacific bases and new terminals in Miami and San Francisco, Juan Trippe focused on his long-held dream—flying mail and passengers across the Atlantic to Europe.

The planned northern route would begin in Baltimore, continuing on to New York City; Shediac, New Brunswick; Botwood, Newfoundland; and across the Atlantic to Foynes, Ireland (see chapter 13). The Clippers would terminate the Atlantic crossing at Imperial Airways' flying boat facilities in Southampton, England.

In 1930, Newark, New Jersey, was the major East Coast airport, but it was incompatible for flying boat operations. This was of little concern to Trippe. Across the Hudson Bay was where he wanted his terminal—in New York City. To this end, he would soon find himself allied with New York's colorful mayor, Fiorello H. LaGuardia, who was equally intent on an airport that would service the metropolis.

Mayor LaGuardia had once refused to leave his aircraft when it landed at Newark. "I paid for a ticket to New York City, and it clearly states that fact, not Newark, New Jersey," he told the press.

Elected in 1934, LaGuardia immediately began a massive transportation improvement campaign, which included large amounts

of federal Works Progress Administration funds for highways, bridges, tunnels, and a mass transit system. In addition, LaGuardia understood the need for a major airport, not only to service a large metropolitan area, but also to stimulate the economy.

A few years prior, Trippe had used runways at the Glenn Curtis Airport at North Beach on Long Island Bay when piloting his own small aircraft to East Hampton. Trippe knew that airport, which closed in 1929, would be the most ideal location.

Trippe and LaGuardia joined forces, and on September 3, 1937, they broke ground for the new airport after President Roosevelt approved the purchase and plans for the site. At $40 million, LaGuardia Field and the Marine Air Terminal became the most expensive airport in the world. It would encompass 558 acres with nearly four miles of runways and facilities for the giant Clippers to operate.

The same architectural firm that had designed Dinner Key and the prefab buildings for Midway and Wake once again came on board, lending their art deco style to New York's terminal. The circular main portion of the terminal rises into tiers like a wedding cake, forming an open two-story core with wings attached to each side. Clad in brick and limestone, trimmed in white marble with friezes of yellow flying fish on the stonework, it is described in architectural literature as one of the hallmarks of the Delano & Aldrich firm. Murals of marine and aviation motifs splendidly compliment the interior, and just as in Miami and San Francisco, an observation deck tops off the roof. Displayed in the lobby, Pan Am's iconic world globe steals the show.

The oldest existing airport from the "Golden Age of Architecture," the Marine Air Terminal remains part of LaGuardia Airport, albeit with limited use as a hub for shuttle flights to Boston, Washington, Toronto, and Montreal. Nevertheless, it stands as a reminder of an exciting bygone era—a time when high style blended with efficiency and comfort—when impossible dreams came true almost in the blink of an eye.

Just as Trippe envisioned, Pan Am's Dinner Key, Treasure Island, Marine Air Terminal, Wake, Midway, *and* the magnificent Clippers would all be singular, unforgettable experiences.

Rebecca Sprecher
and Dian Groh

"Surely that a flight on a Pan Am Clipper will be remembered as the most romantic voyage in history."

Ike all great periods in history, the era of the flying boats show-cased both substance and style. Their technological achieve-ments notwithstanding, these aircraft also offered an elegant, first-class experience in flight. Juan Trippe had traveled aboard the great ocean liners as a child, and was familiar with the appointments and services that his well-heeled passengers would require. The new Sikorsky models, for example, were the first aircraft to have seats specifically designed for the plane. Until this time, passengers sat in flimsy wicker chairs bolted to the floor. Later models would feature a galley equipped to prepare hot meals—a great improve-ment over cold plates and buffets.

But Trippe was also thinking about how to style the growing airline in a way that would coordinate with the new equipment and create a branding image. During his service in the navy in WWI, he developed a love of all things nautical. Beginning with the Martin aircraft that crossed the Pacific, he transferred this nautical theme to his planes, employing terminology such as starboard and port, forward and aft, galleys, and so forth. It would become the industry standard, and is still in use today. These nautical designations also brought to mind the yachting culture that Trippe's clientele was familiar with and understood. Beginning with the Sikorskys, he decided to call his flying boats "Clippers" after the fast tea-trading sailing ships in the nineteenth century, copyrighting the name for use on all Pan Am aircraft going forward. His pilots wore uniforms modeled after US naval officers, consisting of black wool jackets and pants, white shirts, black ties, and white hats with black brims. After the war, rank was indicated by stripes of gold braid on the sleeves and gold insignia on the brims of the hats.

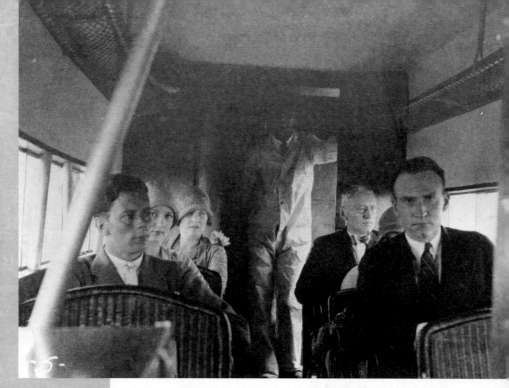

Chief Engineer André Priester was the author of the operations manual that detailed various regulations regarding uniforms, the chain of command, and codes of conduct. As soon as the aircraft doors were closed, the captain assumed absolute command of the aircraft with all the authority and legal powers endowed to a sea captain, including the ability to perform marriages. In addition to being in charge of executing the flight plan or handling an emergency, he could offload an unruly passenger and arbitrate crew disputes. It was the captain who was in charge of ordering and paying for fuel downline. If a high-ranking Pan Am official happened to be on board as a passenger, even he could not question the captain's decisions regarding a maintenance issue or procedures in flight. This policy remains in effect in the airline industry today.

Priester wrote in the Pilot Conduct section of his operations manual that his pilots "should at all times bear in mind that they are representatives of the Company at every point of call, and shall conduct themselves in such manner as to reflect upon the Company." Privately, however, he complained that they were occasionally capable of "hot-blooded panache and acts of daring." Priester also forbade alcohol on Pan Am flights in the early days, but invariably a bottle was brought forth from a passenger's bag to the delight of all. This "no alcohol" policy would go by the wayside with the end of Prohibition in 1933, and the addition of formal meal services, with a full bar and fine wines being provisioned.

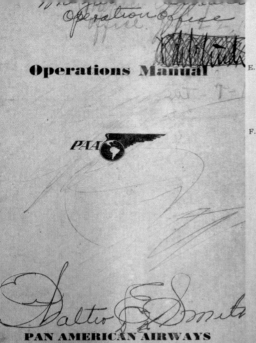

f. Assistance and material required
g. Injuries to persons or damage to property
h. Conditions regarding resumption of flight
i. Precautions taken for the proper guarding and mooring of aircraft.
j. Pilot's communication address.

E. PASSENGERS AND LOAD

25. In addition to the assigned crew of the aircraft no persons except those authorized by ticket or company pass for the particular flight shall be carried.

26. No load or article shall be carried which is prohibited by the Customs, Immigration or Air Traffic laws of any nation included in the flight.

F. PILOT'S CONDUCT

27. Pilots shall at all times bear in mind that they are representatives of the Company at every point of call, and shall conduct themselves in such manner as to reflect credit upon the Company.

28. It is the responsibility of the pilot to thoroughly acquaint himself with the air, traffic, field and hangar rules at each point of call on his schedule and to conform to those rules.

29. Pilots are encouraged to freely make suggestions and recommendations for the improvement of the Company Service. Such suggestions and recommendations shall be made in writing to the Division Operations Manager who shall cause a copy thereof to be appended to the record of the pilot concerned.

30. The pilot shall supply himself with sufficient funds to cover probable expenses of the flight. When necessary requisition for flight funds shall be made through the Operations Manager or the Airport Manager.

Disbursement and accounting of flight funds shall be as required by the office of the Comptroller.

9

But without a doubt, Pan Am's style became firmly established in the public imagination with the debut of the Boeing 314, the greatest flying boat of all. Comfort would become more important than ever, particularly for long overnight crossings of the Atlantic that could last twenty-four hours. The efficiency of the big plane lay with its twin decks, one for passengers, the other one for crew and cargo.

The interior design for the Boeing 314 was dreamy indeed, inspired by the tranquil themes of ocean, constellations, and twilight. New York interior designer Norman Bel Geddes, an art deco enthusiast, was selected to head the team for the Boeing 314. Bel Geddes understood the design rule that form follows function, and nowhere was it more appropriate than on an airplane, where weight and safety were paramount considerations. For example, since the plane was unpressurized, he used a new material called Plexiglas on the windows rather than glass, and lightweight but durable seat cushions were made of Australian horsehair mixed with latex. Designer Howard Ketcham was hired to develop fabric and color selections that would reflect the seas and skies, finding ideal combinations and intensities. While the cabin needed to reflect light and create a feeling of openness, the colors could not be too bright,

1. . Lining - gold beige, cotton, Jacquard design (PAA Map). No. 8163, 50" wide, .3#/ sq. yd. F. Schumacher & Co. h.y.

2. . Lining - Plain gold beige cotton, #8164, 50" wide, .3 lbs./sq. yd. F. Schumacher & Co. h.y.

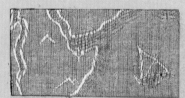

3. . Lining - Light green, cotton fabric with Jacquard design # A8165, 50" wide, .3 lbs./sq. yd. F. Schumacher & Co. h.y.

4. . Lining - Dark green, all wool mohair, plain, #A190, 50" wide, .48 lbs./sq.yd. L. C. Chase + Co. h.y.

5. Upholstery - Tan all wool tapestry fabric, #11332 Color 50, 54" wide, .76 lbs./sq. yd. Johnson + Faulkner, h.y.

6. & 7. Upholstery - Plain blue cotton tapestry #12910 Color 30, 54" wide, 92 lbs./sq. yd. Figures blue cotton tapestry #11538 Color 30, 54" wide, 1.06 lbs./sq.yd. Moss Rose Mfg. Co.
8. Ticking - No sample. See specifications.

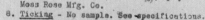

9. Carpet - Receda Green Seamloc Broadloom, quality #50734, Color 38, 2.4 lbs./sq. yd. L. C. Chase. h.y.

10. Carpet - Rose beige Seamloc broadloom, quality #50734, Color 32, 2.4 lbs./sq. yd. L. C. Chase + Co. h.y.

lest they strain the eyes while aloft for long periods of time. If they were too pale or drab, the passengers might find the experience dull and insufficiently luxurious. It was a delicate assignment, but Ketcham eventually settled on two different palettes for the seating compartments. "Miami Beige" walls and terra-cotta carpet alternated with "Skyline Green" walls and carpet in a medium blue shade they called "Pan American Blue." (Pan Am Blue would become a familiar term from that day forward, the shade varying slightly according to new styling requirements.) Floor coverings were created by L. C. Chase and Company, whose works now appear in the Metropolitan Museum of Art in New York.

Interior fabrics for the B-314 were provided by various prominent houses, such as Schumacher, a company whose products graced everything from the Waldorf Astoria Hotel in New York and the Breakers in Palm Beach to the wallpaper for Tara in *Gone With the Wind*. Carpets and upholstery needed to be lightweight but absorb sound, and all fabrics were required to be flame-proofed by the manufacturers. The lounge and dining areas were more relaxed and convivial, with seats covered in dark-blue material sprinkled with gold stars. In most other areas of the aircraft, the walls and ceilings were covered in soft-textured fabrics to mitigate noise. The overall atmosphere of the cabins was one of beauty, calm, and understated elegance.

The agreed-upon fabric for the flight deck was a dark-green mohair blend, which enhanced night vision for the pilots, both to monitor their instruments, and to "shoot the stars" for navigational purposes.

Pan Am passengers during this era were the crème de la crème of American and European society, and there was only one class of service on the flying boats—first class. Naturally, they dressed the part. What to wear in this new world of aviation was very much on the mind of one such passenger, Betsy Schafer, who had accepted the assignment of writing an article for *Vogue* about her upcoming trip aboard the *Atlantic Clipper* on July 5, 1939:

"When my husband first came home with the news that we were flying the Atlantic, I suddenly realized that I wasn't the type. Before he had finished his self-important explanation of how difficult it was to get on the first crossings, I had my hair clipped close in the back, short over the ears and just long enough on top to dangle boyishly over my forehead. Blue was my color, so slacks in that becoming shade, of course. (Trousers are a necessity, my dear, don't be silly!) I knew how high one has to step sometimes into a plane and somehow I seemed to see myself on a wing, repairing an engine or plugging a leak."

Schafer's wardrobe deliberations took on a more serious tone after she read a *New York Times* article indicating that she and her husband might be invited to sit at the prestigious captain's table.

"I was stunned! Aboard the 'Clipper' one could manage a long dress? ... Within a minute I was visualizing that Bonwit number with the Stop Red chiffon scarf. But somehow that wasn't dramatic enough. After all, there hadn't been many women ahead of me to fly the Atlantic, and it seemed a pity not to do the unusual. Perhaps I could persuade Hawes [designer Elizabeth Hawes] to do something in airplane silk (Pan Am Archives)!"

Schafer needn't have worried about wardrobe changes. She could easily change from casual traveling clothes into an elegant gown in the ladies' powder room. Spacious and well-equipped, it featured a sink with hot and cold running water, a dressing table, two swivel stools covered in turquoise leather, and a large mirror with flattering lighting. Custom-designed accordion window shades, created by the Claude D. Carver Company in New York, coordinated with the color schemes of additional window shades throughout the passenger cabins. And if anyone had the indelicacy to ask, the aircraft's toilets and washbasins were designed to release waste material outside into the atmosphere.

Already a member of New York's high society, Betsy Schafer now found herself elevated to the object of unbridled jealousy. As word traveled about her unprecedented flight, she found her status immeasurably enhanced with invitations from fellow socialites, accompanied by gushing exclamations. "You know, she is crossing on the Clipper. Isn't it thrilling, my dears?" Betsy was also the envious target of women she didn't even know. Longing to rub elbows with a Pan Am passenger of Betsy's social rank, many would have thought or said, "Oh, how I envy you. If only I could go in your place."

As a result, prior to the momentous flight, Schafer took great care not to endanger her passage, going to the extent of physical training, even denying herself customary evening cocktails . . . for at least two days. She took care not to catch cold or slip in the bathtub, and insisted her cabdrivers take extra caution. "I'm flying the Atlantic!" she explained.

When at last it came time to depart, Schafer and her fellow passengers gathered at Pan Am's office on 42nd Street to board a special bus that would transport them to the Clipper's berth at Port Washington on Long Island. One of her friends who had come to see her off observed, "Well, it doesn't make any difference whether I see you again or not. You will never have more orchids on your chest, dead or alive" (Pan Am Archives).

War Service

Theodore C. "Ted" Johnson was hired as one of 200 stewards in January 1943, and was based at San Francisco's Treasure Island to assist with the war effort. His Pan Am career spanned more than forty years in onboard passenger service. In an oral history contained within the Louis Turpin Aviation Archives at the San Francisco Airport Museum, Ted preserved history by recording his military days of flying the B-314.

Ted Johnson. *Courtesy of the Johnson Family*

> "Gone were the cart service and seven-course meals. Our passengers were all military on a mission. In both the Martin and Boeing aircraft we had steam tables, which, believe it or not, were heated by a line that ran from the engine all the way to the steam table. It was full of antifreeze, and that would raise the temperature to 140 or 150 degrees Fahrenheit. That was enough to serve hot meals and to make coffee or tea. Canned juice was provided as liquid refreshment. After the meal, both stewards converted the passenger seats into sleeping berths, six beds in each compartment. Stanchions attached to the seats created the support for the upper bunk. Seat cushions formed the lower mattress; backs, the upper one. We put on sheets and pillowcases, handed out blankets, lowered the blinds at the windows so it would stay dark and opened the curtains on the aisle so passengers could enter.
>
> Although I did fly Roosevelt's Cabinet to Honolulu to meet with MacArthur, including his adviser Harry Hopkins while the president traveled by cruiser, and had an exciting adventure flying on one engine with Joseph Farrington of Hawaii, my flying boat passengers were primarily military. It was a marvelous machine!"

Confident as Schafer had been up to this point, she suddenly found herself more than a little nervous. Walking down the long pier toward the impressive *Atlantic Clipper*, she likened herself to an animal being led to slaughter. "Stiff upper lip," she muttered. "Jeanne d'Arc and the stake have nothing on the little woman [this] day."

The gong sounded once, initiating the flight crew's military-style boarding march. Moments later, the anticipated second gong signaled that passengers could proceed to the airship. The ceremonial boarding procedures were reassuring to nervous passengers like Schafer. After all, few people had ever flown across a vast ocean, and most everyone around the world knew this was only Pan Am's second Atlantic crossing using the southern route.

Soon after being shown to their seats by attentive stewards, the four engines sputtered briefly, then roared to life. Like it or not, Schafer realized she was now committed to the journey:

> "The door was closed. Locked. The safety belts tightened. It was too late now. We taxied across the Bay. The ship was turned into the wind. The motors were tested. That moment of hesitation before the throttle is opened wide. I looked about me, willing to give strength through my eyes to the faint-hearted, and discovered two men playing a game of rummy!! I turned away quickly and couldn't help but see the man opposite me fingering the open pages of 'Can We Save Democracy.' Damn awkward thing to be saving at a time like this (Pan Am Archives)."

And then began one of "the most casual, calm, and matter-of-fact trips" Schafer had ever experienced. "From the moment we left the water, it became an easing off, a relaxing of the tension I had built up on land." By the time the stewards began serving luncheon, she barely realized that they were passing over Nantucket, their last sight of land until they reached the Azores.

Service on board the Clipper was professional, gracious, and worthy of the station of the passengers. During meal services, flight stewards wore uniforms reminiscent of crews on the ocean liners—formal white jackets of white duck material. Stewards were charged with ordering the food, supervising its delivery to the aircraft, and preparing it once aloft. Dining tables were covered in white Irish linen, with appropriate European crystal for wines, champagne, and cocktails, and meals were served on white bone china adorned with the Pan Am logo. Bel Geddes had designed suction bottoms for the plates and saucers to keep them from moving around during turbulence. The gleaming silver cutlery was in the "Moderne" pattern by Gorham, and the coffee and tea service was silver plate. The layout for the four-by-

Before the Boeing 314s became the hallmark of elegant travel, passengers and crewmembers had to possess an intrepid and adventurous spirit. The first commercial "boats" Pan Am operated were noisy, vibrating, unheated, unpressurized, and uncomfortable, yet it was these very Sikorsky S-38 models that pioneered routes to Central and South America from Pan Am's base in Miami.

Joe "Joey" Carrero was hired as one of the first five Pan Am flying boat stewards at the age of twenty-one. He flew for more than eleven years out of Miami, logging 2,173,200 miles and eighteen months in the air. Thanks to his grandson, Kenny Slagle, and a 1977 article from the now defunct Miami News, his memories offer glimpses into the days before Boeing glamour.

> *"When we first began using the flying boats, it took us nine days to go between Miami and Buenos Aires, flying by day and laying over at night. The engines were so noisy you had to write notes to be understood and nobody had much appetite for eating.*
>
> *Meals? We didn't even offer them at first. Food was a problem. I'd go to the supermarket in Miami before we'd take off and buy provisions for the crew—canned goods, crackers, bread, soups. But for the passengers—and we were never more than half full—we'd pick up box lunches whenever we landed. It wasn't the most comfortable trip you could take, that's for sure."*

four-foot galley called for a drip coffee maker, overhead lighting, a ten-by-twelve-inch sink for washing dishes, and a combination stove and steamer. The sixteen-gauge aluminum icebox contained food items, which was removable for restocking at the airports.

After luncheon, Schafer and the other passengers began retiring to their compartments to take naps or read. Although she doesn't mention it in her notes, she and her husband might indeed have been invited to the captain's table for dinner, for which she most certainly could have worn her "airplane silk" dress. The lounge would have been converted into a dining room for twelve at three tables of four, plus two smaller serving tables. To accommodate all passengers and crew, there were three dinner seatings on overnight flights at 6:00, 7:30, and 9:00 p.m.

Dinner might have consisted of turtle soup followed by a main course of filet mignon, asparagus with hollandaise sauce, and mashed potatoes. Following the order for a formal service in France, salad would have been served afterward, then a cheese and fruit course, dessert, coffee, and *petit fours*. After dinner, the furniture could be quickly stowed, transforming the room back into a lounge where passengers could enjoy card games and conversation, and sip after-dinner drinks.

PAA Logo Dinner service set on board the Boeing 314. Courtesy of PAHF.

Meanwhile, the stewards would prepare the compartments for sleeping, much like Pullman cars. Beds were made up with pale-blue sheets and darker gray-blue blankets, the latter adorned with the Pan Am logo. Full-length privacy curtains in Pan Am blue attached to a decorative frame on the ceiling with snap fasteners. A triangular opening was left in the middle, like a tent. Once the passenger was inside, the curtain could be fastened shut, each bunk with its own window, reading light, and air vent. Other appointments included a clothes hanger, shelf, and steward call button. Passengers assigned to a top bunk found a small stepladder placed close by. The starboard

Boeing 314 Sleeper berths. *Courtesy of PAHF.*

compartment berths were positioned in the horizontal direction from starboard to port, and slept four on two upper and lower bunks. On the port side, one upper and one lower berth were situated in the forward/aft direction. The full complement of passengers was seventy-four, but on long overnight flights requiring sleeping berths, the number varied from thirty-two to forty.

For those desiring extra pampering and privacy, a bridal or honeymoon suite was located at the rear. It was elegantly furnished with a davenport that could be made up into comfortable upper and lower sleeping berths, black walnut side tables, and a writing

table covered with leather. A vanity with a stool and mirror concealed a sink, and a closet was available for the passengers' wardrobes. On Schafer's flight, a pair of newlyweds did indeed occupy the bridal suite. They would disembark at Horta in the Azores before the *Atlantic Clipper* flew on to Lisbon.

Catering to important and influential people was a strategic marketing plan, intended to increase Pan Am's exposure. To add value to the high cost of Clipper airfares, it was essential for passengers like Schafer to revel in highly positive experiences—to write about them, and spread the word through firsthand accounts. It worked. As Pan Am's business steadily grew, so did its reputation and stature. Even if early Clipper travel was affordable only to the wealthy upper echelons of society, eventually Pan American evolved into the airline of choice, fulfilling Trippe's long-term goal of reaching the "everyman."

During the next several years, Pan Am's style and prestige became known the world over. Hollywood directors didn't hesitate to put the airline in their films. In the 1933 production *Flying Down to Rio*, dancers performed on the wing of a Sikorsky. Three years later, Humphrey Bogart starred in *China Clipper* along with Pat O'Brien.

When Bette Davis bids Paul Henreid a tearful farewell in Rio in the 1942 production of *Now, Voyager*, a Sikorsky S-42 sits waiting in the background, propellers twirling. Alfred Hitchcock's *Notorious* was released in 1946, and although there are no specific images of a Pan Am logo, a scene does take place on an airplane where Carey Grant's cover is that of a Pan Am vice president.

When WWII began, these planes became more than just winged silver carriages for the rich and famous. Pan Am delivered invaluable services, transporting Allied commanders and statesmen, royalty, spies, medicines for the Red Cross, mail, and war material. This, too, was the subject of Hollywood movies. Singer Jane Froman was en route to Europe on the *Yankee Clipper* to entertain the troops when the aircraft caught a wingtip while landing on the Tagus River in Lisbon and crashed. She survived the impact, but was severely injured. Crewman John Burn, who had been injured himself, managed to keep her afloat until they were rescued, and several years later they married. A movie titled *With a Song in My Heart*, starring Susan Hayward and Rory Calhoun, was made about their story.

But perhaps the ultimate statement of Pan Am's importance during the war can be found in the film *Casablanca*, in this exchange between Captain Reynault (Claude Rains) and saloonkeeper Rick Blaine (Humphrey Bogart):

Reynault: "That's the plane to Lisbon. You would like to be on it."

Rick: "Why? What's in Lisbon?"

Reynault: "The Clipper to America."

It was simply assumed that everybody who heard that line knew what "the Clipper" was. Pan Am was now a symbol of the United States and of freedom. It was the embodiment of American ingenuity and prosperity, a beacon of hope in a war-torn world.

Schafer crossed the Atlantic at the very beginning of what would become a golden age in Pan Am's history, the age of the "dreamboats." Flying was now perceived to be fast, safe, and comfortable. And it all came about in an era when travel was an art rather than a chore, when style and elegance transformed what could have been a long, arduous ocean crossing into a voyage of romance. When the *Atlantic Clipper* landed in Lisbon, Schafer described it as effortless and magical, the plane literally "gliding into the harbor." Her next emotion was one of euphoria: "For twenty-four hours we had been in a world all our own. This was Europe! It was difficult for the brain to grasp (Pan Am Archives)."

This thrill of travel that Schafer described was exactly what Trippe was after. In his mind, he could see an industry being born, with enormous potential as equipment became more advanced. While such onboard luxury would not be repeated in the coming years of shorter flights and mass travel, the flying boats had served their purpose. For it was these very special aircraft that made the Pan Am dream come true—for Trippe and for the world.

Flying Back in Time

Rebecca Snider Sprecher
with Dian Stirn Groh

CHAPTER 12

"Time is a sort of river of passing events, and strong is its current; no sooner is a thing brought to sight than it is swept by and another takes its place."

—Marcus Aurelius Antonius

Preserving history is no easy task. Big events that seem larger than life when they happen can become fragile when information about them is scattered and lost forever. Memories fade, facts blur, generations move on, seemingly insignificant items and documents are neglected or lost. While we all know that preserving buildings, art and artifacts, letters and memorabilia is important, the history of a business hasn't always registered in the public's mind as a hot ticket item worthy of saving. But thanks to the foresight of a small group of former Pan Am employees, this great airline's historic corporate records and artifacts were not only saved, they were kept together. The monumental task was accomplished by the formation of a nonprofit organization called the Pan Am Historical Foundation (PAHF) that would provide the legal entity through which these items could be acquired.

During bankruptcy legal proceedings on October, 6, 1992, Pan Am asked the court to authorize the "abandonment of certain unnecessary and burdensome records," essentially freeing them up to be sold at auction. (Internal corporate records, such as environmental and tax reports, personnel files, and other financial and legal documents were not included.) At the bankruptcy auction, PAHF and the University of Miami jointly purchased more than 85,000 boxes of material. Of these, 7,385 boxes were deemed appropriate for keeping. More than a hundred Pan Am employees then reviewed and organized these

materials again and again. They were aided and guided by personnel from the Richter Library Special Collections at the University of Miami.

The Pan Am collection—some 1,600 acid-free boxes of paper, photographic, and audiovisual records— is by far the largest of its kind at Richter Library. Extremely valuable documents, such as the original handwritten letters from Charles Lindbergh to Juan Trippe, are kept in an additionally secured area on the Special Collections floor and can be viewed only in the presence of the Special Collections librarian. Three-dimensional objects were placed with the History Miami Museum and the Smithsonian in Washington.

As former Pan Am flight attendants, Dian Groh and I had visited other places featuring our company's history. The impressive museum at the San Francisco International Airport displays beautifully framed oil paintings of Pan Am's historic planes at memorable destinations, along with flight attendant uniforms and a first-cover stamp collection.

We found Pan Am's first mail plane and Juan Trippe's iconic giant globe at the Smithsonian Flight and Air Museum in Washington, DC. At Houston's 1940 Air Terminal, we were delighted to see an eclectic exhibit of Pan Am memorabilia.

Still, we wanted more—to see and touch our history up close and personal. We'd heard about the Pan Am archives in Miami, so perhaps it was time to go there. But would the documents we might find illuminate additional aspects about the company we'd worked for, or would it just be a rehash of what we'd already read in the many fine books written about it? There was so much we didn't know.

Dian and I live in different parts of the US mainland, and had not met until the 2015 World Wings Convention of former Pan Am flight attendants in Savannah. We were put in touch via mutual friend and fellow stewardess Teresa Webber, who was hatching the concept for this book from her home in the Hawaiian Islands. She asked if Dian and I would visit the Richter Library and report back about any flying boat "treasures" we uncovered. It would be an endeavor of stewardess synergy and cross-country research.

This kind of task seemed familiar, because forming immediate relationships with flight crews we'd never met had been the accepted routine. Complete strangers would report for pre-flight briefings and volunteer for assignments to staff emergency exits and conduct meal services. Once on board, we performed our jobs like a well-oiled machine, putting passengers at ease and ensuring their comfort. Though always prepared for the unexpected, we facilitated a smooth, efficient flow of service that was calm and professional.

While the passengers slept, we congregated in the galleys, often revealing personal life stories. During layovers at down-line destinations, we absorbed fascinating cultures and shared many adventures. By the time we returned to our home bases, we were the best of friends. Such was the crew culture we'd been a part of, so it was not unusual when Dian and I arranged to visit Miami without ever having laid eyes on one another. Already we were touching the river of time in our own pasts as well as that of Pan American's.

Before starting out on the seven-hour drive to Miami, we knew our main area of interest would be focused on the golden age of the flying boats. Another reason for the trip was to write about the experience of accessing the archives. But for me, there was yet another reason, one that was personal.

I grew up with some wildly entertaining cousins by marriage who often mentioned a distant relative named Bill Winston. Other than the fact that he was a pilot for Pan Am during WWII, little was known about him. I had not seen his name in any of the books I'd read, but maybe I could find material on him in the archives, gain a sense of his personality, and report back to the family. Most likely he was a calm, cerebral type like my uncle, a lawyer and Civil War scholar. These cousins of mine, on the other hand, were cut from a different cloth. We spent our summer vacations together in Wilmington, North Carolina, in a boisterous delirium, exploring then-uninhabited Figure Eight Island. By day, we learned how to swear and play cards; by night, how to trip the light fantastic. They grew up to be expert seamen and rapscallions, tooting off on bourbon-soaked fishing trips, and remarkably, making their way home in gale-force winds. For decades, the whole family wondered from what genetic pool these high-spirited characters sprang. Perhaps the archives would be able to shed some light on the mystery, but it was a long shot. After all, with more than 1,600 boxes, it would be like looking for the proverbial needle in a haystack.

A few weeks before arriving at the Richter, Dian and I researched the Special Collections website, trying to determine which boxes might contain the flying boat information we were seeking. It was a daunting task, but fortunately, in 2012, a two-year cataloging effort supported by a grant from the National Historical Publications and Records Commission enabled these materials to be organized into eighteen thematic series with more than 300 subthemes to aid in searching the collection. The system for organizing subject matter was devised by analyzing folder titles and by examining their contents, which was then made available for online searches.

After arriving in Miami, we settled into a Coconut Grove hotel and immediately reverted to our crew culture. Over dinner and cocktails, we relived many of the worldwide places we'd been so fortunate to visit. Besides Teresa, it was no surprise we had several Pan Am friends in common. The next morning, we stepped out of the elevator on the eighth floor of the library promptly at nine o'clock, and were shown to lockers where we could leave our belongings. Jay Sylvestre, Special Collections librarian, instructed us on the procedure for inspecting the contents of the boxes and provided white cotton gloves for handling photographs. Waiting for the boxes to arrive, our fertile imaginations conjured a final scene from *Raiders of the Lost Ark*. We envisioned stacks of dusty boxes being wheeled through a dark, cavernous warehouse by a bent, elderly man who absentmindedly brushed by priceless treasures along the way. Hollywood ideas quickly vanished when it was explained that the Pan Am bequest is located off campus in a climate-controlled warehouse. Requested materials are efficiently selected and trucked to the library's carefully monitored examination room.

A staffer wheeled in the first cart with six boxes. Opening each box would be akin to Christmas morning. The excitement we felt

was palpable. Finally, we hoped, we were going to discover the behind-the-scenes history of one of the most glamorous, elegant, and important eras in the annals of aviation!

We began going through one box after another, handling each file tenderly, as if they were eggshells. The first ones documented the building of Pan Am's down-line Pacific stations on Canton, New Caledonia, Midway, and Wake in the 1930s. We chuckled at a candid photograph of suntanned, shirtless young men playing golf in the sand on Midway, golf bags slung over their bare shoulders with the island's ubiquitous gooney birds curiously trailing behind them.

Soon we came across the October 14, 1935, issue of the *Guam Eagle,* a homegrown newspaper mimeographed on eight-and-a-half-by-eleven-inch paper. We could almost hear the Underwood keys clattering as a secretary typed from a wooden desk, a ceiling fan twirling slowly overhead. On page fifteen were college football scores. Notre Dame had trounced Wisconsin, 27-0. UCLA had beaten Stanford in a squeaker, 7-6. We were amazed that on that distant island, such close attention was paid to college football games in the '30s.

But it was the cover story that jumped out at us—the arrival of a Pan Am Clipper proving flight, a Sikorsky S-42 with Capt. R.O.D. Sullivan in command. The forerunners to mail and passenger flights, proving flights were essential to confirm navigation procedures and verify flight times and fuel consumption. Because extra fuel tanks filled the cabins, passengers were never carried. Nevertheless, the Clipper's arrival was big news, as the reporter vivified:

"Persons familiar with the pleasant routine of life in Guam could not [help] but observe even at an early hour that yesterday [Sunday] was to be a day of unusual import. Automobiles, bicycles, carabaos (water buffalo), bull carts and outrigger canoes from all parts of the island were converging on the Pan American Airport at Sumay. Rumbling trucks with huge trailers, all loaded with school children, boy scouts and girl scouts, joined in the one-way procession . . ."

Capt. George A. Alexander, USN and governor of Guam, officially welcomed the flight, followed by a two-hour reception for 400 invited guests at Government House. There is no question that the people of Guam knew the importance of such an occasion beyond just watching an airplane land in their harbor. Whether the writer intended to capitalize the word "isolation" is unclear; if so, it speaks volumes to how they felt about what was happening:

"3:12 p.m., Sunday, 13 October, 1935 marks a turning point in the history of Guam. Guam has stepped out of the era of Isolation and is now entering upon an era of extensive possibilities, an era in which she will be one of the important stepping stones in the commerce of the Air between the United States and the Orient. By this conquest of the air the relative size of the earth has again become smaller and Guam finds herself among closer neighbors."

We were struck by this account, because it was too small a story to rate mentioning in most history books. Only in an archival setting can one fully access such accounts, which generate intimate and emotional relationships between the material and the viewer. Gazing at the hand-drawn diagram of the Pan Am plane, we could imagine ourselves living there during that time, even working on the newspaper ourselves.

On we went through the first box until we reached the last folder. In it was a clipping from a Long Beach, California, newspaper dated December 15, 1942, documenting an incident that flight engineer Sylvester Tunis had experienced on board the *Pacific Clipper*, the same Boeing 314 that Capt. Bob Ford had taken around the world in reverse after the bombing of Pearl Harbor. According to the article, the Clipper was taxiing toward her mooring (presumably at Fisherman's Lake, Liberia) when "a sudden gust of wind drove the ship against an uncharted reef, where she grounded hard." Sounded interesting, I thought, preparing to slip the article back into the folder.

Then a name jumped out at me. "Captain William A. Winston finally wormed the 84,000-pound plane off the reef and taxied her to the shelter of the shore." That *had* to be him!

The article went on to explain that the hull had been ripped wide open. Two of her main compartments were flooded with murky water, and no possibility of rescue was in sight. Soon after the damage was assessed, passengers were rerouted on other flights. Facing an enormous challenge, Capt. Winston knew it would take teamwork, inventive thinking, and the use of only what was on hand to make the necessary repairs. And so began another chapter in Pan Am's untold story.

To begin underwater repairs, the stranded crew first needed to improvise a diving helmet. Under the direction of Flight Engineer William Miller, who had arrived on an inbound flight, a hole was cut in a five-gallon flour can. Next, for submerged viewing, they attached a custom-cut pane of glass and completed the makeshift helmet by borrowing a hose from the ground crew's welding equipment. Air was delivered via two hand-operated pumps from one of the station's trucks. The area floodlit by the headlights from another truck, the *Pacific Clipper's* crew worked continuous four-man shifts in mud, seven feet below the surface, by day and long into the coming nights.

To keep the compartments dry while water was pumped out, a tarpaulin was painstakingly maneuvered beneath the keel, at which point metal plates were attached to the ripped hull using 1,000 screws, 300 hundred of them hand-drilled.

Finally came the most daunting task of all. Braced with two-by-four African timbers, 1,500 pounds of cement was hand-mixed and poured into the damaged compartments. Under seemingly impossible odds, after only one week, Winston and his exhausted crew completed their 6,000-mile scheduled flight to New York.

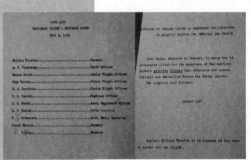

Atlantic Clipper (B-314A) crew list and PR blurb about the Irish prime minister aboard. Courtesy of the Pan Am Archives, University of Miami, Richter Library.

Once I had Winston's complete name, the equipment he was on (the 314), and his division (the Atlantic), the Special Collections staff was able to do a more detailed computer search and find another box containing files with more information.

Fellow pilot Horace Brock wrote in his book *Flying the Oceans*, that he didn't much like Winston until he began to regale Brock with stories and play the piano on a layover at the Estoril Palace Hotel near Lisbon, Portugal. Another file revealed that Winston was in command of the Atlantic Clipper on July 5, 1939, for Pan Am's second Atlantic crossing using the southern route through the Azores. Also in the file was the menu for breakfast, the crew list, a newspaper photograph of the departure from Port Washington on Long Island, and notes on the crossing for a *Vogue* article written by passenger Betsy Schafer. The prime minister of Ireland was one of the dignitaries traveling on this flight.

Yet another file turned up information that placed Winston and his crew at the Ikoyi Staff House in Lagos, Nigeria. Eating curry and drinking gin and tonics to ward off malaria, they awaited a special assignment from Pan Am operations. This would have been one of the many Special Missions that Pan Am flew during WWII, missions that traversed both commercial air routes and others not authorized by the Civil Aeronautics Board. In the Atlantic Division, fifty-seven of these ninety-seven missions operated between North Beach field in New York (later renamed LaGuardia Airport) and Fisherman's Lake, Liberia and/or Lagos, Nigeria. On board Charter Flight 27, aircraft NC06 (NC18606, the *American Clipper*) was air photoreconnaissance specialist Maj. Elliot Roosevelt (son of President Franklin Roosevelt), who was escorting a valuable cargo of war films for the United States Army Air Force. They had landed in Lagos and were told to remain there until further notice. Several days later Pan Am Operations advised Captain Winston of a specific request from the president of the United States to transport King George II of Greece and his entourage to Baltimore, Maryland, via Port of Spain, Trinidad. They arrived on schedule and without incident.

Over the course of the next two days, we opened boxes and files containing other treasures: the Navigator's Log of the *China Clipper* and Capt. Ed Musick's personal scrapbook; the text from a speech on the design of the 314 by Boeing engineer Wellwood Beall; the program for the launch of the *Yankee Clipper*; original letters written by Charles Lindbergh to Juan Trippe, and on and on. But perhaps the most gratifying and sobering moment came when I pulled out a series of documents detailing the important people who had flown on the Clippers during WWII. Dian and I were familiar with the statement, "We couldn't have won the war without Pan Am," and that the 314s flew "military brass, diplomats, royalty, and spies" back and forth across the Atlantic. But the true scope of this effort couldn't be fully comprehended until we saw not only the lists of the names, but the reasons for their journeys.

We looked at these pages and gasped. Everybody who was anybody was on the lists:

The entire Allied command structure at one time or another went back and forth to meetings in Washington and Europe; diplomats and royalty traveled to Washington to report on conditions in their countries; ladies and gentlemen of the press flew over to report on the war to a world hungry for information. Harry Hopkins, special adviser to President Roosevelt, flew to London for important meetings, sometimes accompanied by Gen. George C. Marshall. Undersecretary of State Edward Stettinius attended Lend Lease meetings in that city. Darryl Zanuck, then a major in the Signal Corps and later a Hollywood film producer, went over to direct army film projects in England and North Africa. In May 1942, Charlotte, Grand Duchess of Luxembourg, boarded in Foynes, Ireland, to visit President Roosevelt in Washington in the interests of her nation, as did Olav, Crown Prince of Norway. Wilhelm Munthe De Morgenstierne, Norwegian ambassador to the US, returned through Foynes after consultations with his government in exile in London. Gen. Joseph Stillwell flew into Lagos on his way to take over his command in the Far East. Lt. Gen. Dawson Olmstead, Brig. Gen. Roger Carlton, and Maj. Gen. John Downing all flew the Clippers to the United Kingdom for meetings to plan the Africa Invasion.

And then there were the war's storytellers: Clare Luce transited through Lagos on her way to Chunking to interview Mme. Chiang Kai-Shek for *Time* magazine. Ernie Pyle began his assignment as a war correspondent when he traveled on the Clipper to Foynes. Edward R. Murrow flew over through Lisbon en route to start his nightly broadcast from England for the Columbia Broadcasting System. Photographer Margaret Bourke-White from *Time*; Arthur Sulzberger, publisher of the *New York Times*; Joe Alex Morris of United Press International; Lord William Camrose, publisher of the *London*

Telegraph; Mrs. Agnes Meyer, wife of the publisher of the *Washington Post*, all went to observe and document wartime activities and social conditions, as did Henry Taylor of Scripps Howard newspapers, and Time-Life photographer Robert Landry. William S. Paley, president of CBS, went to find out more about radio problems in wartime. Jay Moloney, managing editor of the *Chicago Tribune*, went to Foynes in May of 1944 to report on the invasion push. Mrs. Theodore Roosevelt, director of the American Red Cross clubs in England, was aboard a Clipper in June of 1943. It all left us breathless.

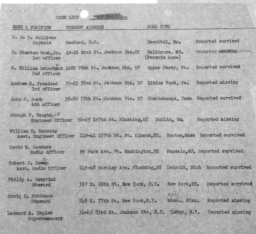

Crew list of *Yankee Clipper* (B-314A) that crashed in Lisbon, Portugal. *Courtesy of the Pan Am Archives, University of Miami, Richter Library.*

At dinner on our last night in Miami, Dian and I reflected on our experience. Perhaps it was the intimacy of two new friends privately viewing these precious bits of history as opposed to seeing them on public display in a museum, but the impact was profound. Indeed, some moments were very sad, such as coming across the crew list from the *Yankee Clipper* crash in Lisbon. The words "reported survived" alternated with "reported missing," indicating the compilation might have been made as details were coming in. In the case of First Officer H. Stanton Rush Jr., the word "missing" had been blacked out and "dead" penciled in small, tightly formed letters beside it. A period beside the word "dead" revealed the grief of the typist, his or her admission of the finality of death, and the emotion of the moment as the tragedy unfolded in real time. We felt like these were our fallen comrades, as indeed, they were. Going through these boxes was like leafing through a family scrapbook belonging to loved ones who had passed on, with both happy and sad occasions to remember.

Captain Winston. *Courtesy of PAHF.*

Dian and I had begun our visit to the archives as strangers, but we were leaving as friends and successful treasure-seekers, enriched by the journey we had just made together, eternally grateful that these materials had been preserved for the future. We felt like we knew our company better than ever before. I also realized there was a family in North Carolina that would soon be stunned by my discovery of Capt. Bill Winston.

For I can now tell my cousins, all of whom are card sharks and accomplished raconteurs capable of keeping a boat afloat on any ocean, that they did not come by these talents at random. Winston was not only a colorful individual who lived through some exceptional adventures, but also made a vital contribution to the war effort during a crucially important time in the history of the world. Thanks to the materials contained in the Pan Am archives, they will gain a greater understanding of themselves. Pan Am is now part of their family story from this generation going forward, and they will feel pride that their ancestor flew for the world's greatest airline. You can't put a price on the sharing of this history, both for the families and for those of us who were employees. For now, the Pan Am archives will keep our airline alive, enabling us to touch the river of time and reverse its swift current.

Off the Beaten Track

A Museum Like No Other

Margaret O'Shaughnessy

O n the southern banks of the River Shannon, thirty miles inland from the Atlantic Ocean and twenty-four miles south of Limerick City, lies the village of Foynes, Ireland. Since the middle of the nineteenth century, Foynes has been a thriving seaport. For generations, the town's population seldom exceeded more than 600 residents, but because of its strategic location, Foynes was critical to aviation history.

The arrival of the Great Southern & Western Railway in 1858, plus the construction of the town's first hotel and pub, put Foynes on the map as an important stopover for Irish immigrants bound for North America. They travelled from Foynes on the one-carriage

Foynes Flying Boat Museum. *Courtesy of Foynes Flying Boat Museum.*

train called The Sentinel via Limerick and Cobh, taking rooms and food at the Monteagle Arms. Eighty years later, the same hotel/restaurant became Ireland's flying boat terminal.

Soon after Charles Lindbergh conducted survey flights over the Shannon Estuary in 1933, Pan American founder and president Juan Trippe became convinced that Foynes was the ideal European port for his Clippers' seventeen-hour Atlantic crossings from New York via Newfoundland. By 1937, when reconstruction of the hotel cum terminal began, Foynes was transforming into a major international airbase for services to Pan American, Imperial, and American Export Airlines. Between 1941 and 1943, more than 2,000 flying boats were being tied up at the once-sleepy village. Thousands of passengers transited, and between 1939 and 1943, more than 348,000 pounds of mail were loaded or off-loaded.

Atlantic Flying Boats Routes. *Courtesy of Foynes Flying Boat Museum.*

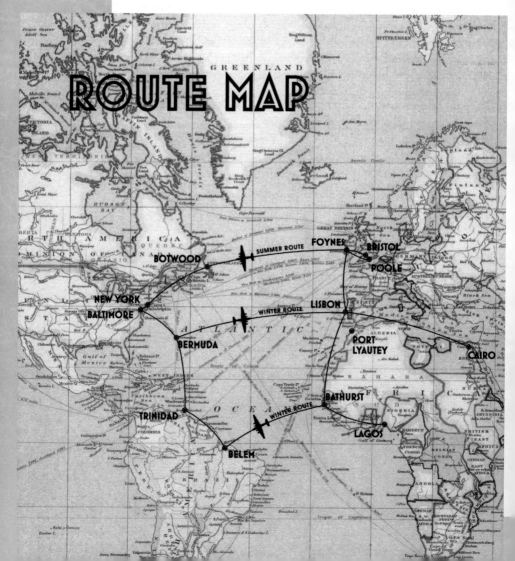

I grew up in the tiny village of Foynes, where I spent a great deal of my youth listening to my grandfather's stories about "airways" and what he called "the great flying boats." I had no idea what flying boats were, nor had I any knowledge of aviation, but many years later, his passions would become mine.

After finishing college, I began work at the Bank of Ireland in Dublin, but city life didn't agree with me. Moving back home in 1973, I was sad to discover my village was even less populated than I remembered. Like I had, most young people moved away to attend university or find work. The last vestige of our town's notoriety was only vaguely recalled when, three decades earlier, the last Pan Am flying boat, the *Pacific Clipper*, had departed Foynes in October 1945.

The terminal closed a year later, and land aircraft began using grass runways at the Shannon airport. Rendered obsolete, flying boats *and* Foynes were all but forgotten.

But in 1981, a chain of events began unfolding that would alter the course of my life, as well as the historical significance of my hometown.

Following a fire at a Dublin nightclub that tragically took the lives of many young people, fire officials were prompted to make close safety inspections of public buildings across Ireland. One structure on the list was the Foynes Parish Hall, an old wooden building doomed to be condemned. Town meetings ensued, and before I knew it, I was elected to a committee.

Our objective was to establish a community council aimed at providing a new center for the citizens of Foynes, and our first goal was to raise the staggering sum of €500,000—about $564,127.50. We organized dances, raffles, swimming competitions, and town festivals until, at last, the brand new Community & Sports Complex opened in 1987.

Impressed with the success of our grassroots fundraising, the Limerick County manager approached me, asking about my future plans. I knew he was hinting at another community project, but I had no idea what he might propose. As we chatted politely, in the back of my mind lingered long-ago conversations with my grandfather—his fascination with aviation, and his love of the "great flying boats."

Without really thinking it through, I suddenly blurted out, "I would like to build an aviation museum to preserve the flying boat history."

And that was how it all began.

By 1988, my enthusiastic nonprofit group of volunteers and I had secured a lease for the site of the museum. Fittingly, it was located in the original terminal building, which had once been the Monteagle Arms Hotel. Utilizing existing historical buildings situated on the shores of our village made perfect sense for our museum. After all,

Foynes had once been the European port of call for all the great flying boats. We had an important history to uphold and perpetuate. Besides that, Ireland had nothing else like it. Our museum would be entirely unique—as it turned out, unlike any other in the world.

We started with four outbuildings consisting of nothing more than mud floors and rock walls. Immediately, we employed architect Brian Grubb and historical interpreter and designer John Harrison. We all agreed flying boats would be the museum's focus.

I first made contact with Pan American through its public relations representatives in Ireland, who suggested I speak with the famous Hollywood movie actress Maureen O'Hara. Her third husband, whom she described as the "love of my life," was none other than Pan Am Chief Pilot Charles Blair. What better publicity for our museum than a Pan Am captain and our very own, Irish-born Maureen O'Hara?

I was amazed at my audacity when I rang her local number in County Cork, where she spent her summers at the scenic portside village of Glengariff. In 1978, Blair had been tragically killed in one of his own Antilles airboats when it crashed in the Caribbean. Having spent the ten years of their marriage travelling the world with "Charlie," O'Hara had a special fondness for all things Pan American. She listened attentively as I explained our museum mission. Then, offering her support, she wholeheartedly encouraged me to stay the course. O'Hara would play a continuous role in the museum's promotion, both at home and overseas as its patron, until her death in October 2015.

Originally, we planned to recreate only one cabin of the Boeing 314, but Harrison had much bigger ideas. After lengthy discussions, he engaged film set designer and model maker Bill Fallover. Both men were adamant that a full-scale replica of an entire B-314 should be built. I believed the skills, talents, and grandiose plans of both men would guarantee the success of the museum as a one-of-a-kind, world-class exhibit. However, the addition of a full-sized B-314 fuselage, replete with all the trimmings, inside and out, would require more funding.

John O'Donoghue, the minister for arts, sports, and tourism, took our proposal seriously. Thanks to his understanding of the museum's historical significance and economic potential, funding was provided, and we enthusiastically commenced work on the project.

Bill Fallover and his amazing team constructed the fuselage compartments in County Wicklow, just south of Dublin. In only ten short months, they completed six passenger cabins, the lounge, upper flight deck, and "bridal suite."

From Wicklow, each fuselage section was trucked 162 miles to Foynes at night in wide loads. Once on site, the sections were lifted into place by large cranes and assembled. The entire process was filmed for a documentary, which is now sold in the museum gift shop.

Over the years, we've acquired all of the original terminal buildings. Considerable expense has gone into restoration and maintenance, as well as exhibit acquisitions, but, by far, the largest portion of funding has been spent on our museum's star attraction, the B-314. In addition to the startling grand size of the fuselage, the interiors of *Yankee Clipper*'s cabins, flight deck, and galley have also been recreated.

Yankee Clipper made worldwide headlines on its inaugural commercial flight from the US when it touched down at Foynes on July 9, 1939. On board were nineteen well-heeled passengers who could easily afford the pricy $675 round-trip fare between New York and Foynes. They had crossed the Atlantic with all the comforts of a first-class ocean liner. The most notable difference was that they had made the crossing in a matter of hours rather than days.

Another of many noteworthy events took place on August 18, 1945, when both the *Atlantic* and *Dixie* Clippers arrived from New York in the morning, and departed that night. One hundred and one transatlantic passengers hailing from Great Britain, Argentina, Sweden, Switzerland, France, Czechoslovakia, the Netherlands, and the USA were given VIP treatment at the Foynes terminal. Other airline companies were also coming and going from Foynes, using different makes and models of flying boats, but they all paled in comparison to the sleek, luxurious, and utterly beautiful Boeing 314.

All of Pan Am's transatlantic galleys were provisioned with 300 pounds of food. Breakfast usually began with fresh strawberries and cream, and for the main meal, stewards in white dinner jackets served shrimp cocktail, turtle soup, fillet steak, mashed potatoes, asparagus, salad, Peach Melba, and *petit fours*. Each course was accompanied by a choice of drinks, but Clipper passengers were especially fond of a Foynes-created beverage initially served only at the terminal.

It was a cold winter night in 1943, when a Clipper flying boat departed Foynes on schedule for Botwood, Newfoundland, en route to its final New York destination. Several hours into the flight, bad weather forced it to turn back. A Morse code message was sent to the Foynes control tower, which was relayed to the terminal's restaurant chef, Joe Sheridan. He and his staff bundled up, returned to work, and began preparing food and drinks for the distressed, shivering passengers. Hoping to assuage their discomfort, Sheridan came up with a brilliant idea. First brewing a dark, rich coffee, he added brown sugar, and then the magic ingredient—Irish whiskey. He topped it off with fresh whipped cream, and Irish coffee was born.

July 8–9, 1989, was the fiftieth anniversary of *Yankee Clipper's* first arrival in Foynes. It was also the grand opening of the Foynes Flying Boat Museum. In usual inimitable style, Pan American

Irish Coffee

Joe Sheridan's creation was such a huge success that it soon became a regular menu item at the terminal, particularly to welcome all VIPs. However, Irish coffee might never have evolved to international fame were it not for travel writer Stanton Delaplane, who passed on the recipe to Jack Koeppler, owner of the Buena Vista Café in San Francisco.

The Buena Vista attempted to recreate it, but without complete success because the chilled topping-off cream sank to the bottom. Determined to perfect the unique quaff with cream floating on top, Koeppler traveled all the way to Rineanna Airport (now Shannon) to master its secret—pouring the cream over the back of a spoon. San Francisco's Buena Vista Café now takes full credit for bringing Irish coffee to the US.

By 1946, the era of flying boats was nearing the end. The once-vital Foynes sea terminal closed as the new wheeled airplanes arrived and departed from Rineanna Airport's runways. Joe Sheridan took his famous drink to Rineanna, where he served it until 1952. He eventually accepted a position with the Buena Vista Café. Regardless of where Sheridan ended up, the real story of Irish coffee is alive and well at the Foynes Flying Boat Museum.

Irish coffee. *Courtesy of Foynes Flying Boat Museum.*

Foynes Museum Irish Coffee Recipe

1. In your Foynes Irish Coffee glass, place an empty teaspoon and fill the glass with boiling water. Allow the water to heat the glass for five seconds.

2. Empty the water. Add one teaspoon brown sugar and a good measure of Irish whiskey.

3. Fill the glass to within one centimeter (almost half an inch) of the brim with very hot, strong black coffee. Stir well to melt all the sugar.

4. Carefully pour lightly whipped cream over the back of a spoon so that it floats on top of the coffee.

5. Do not stir after adding the cream. The true flavor is obtained by drinking the hot coffee and Irish whiskey through the cream.

6. Now, sit back, relax, and enjoy, or, as we say in Ireland, *Slainte!*

Maureen O'Hara Memorabilia Donated to Foynes Museum

(Courtesy of the *Limerick Leader*, July 24, 2016)

Plans are being drawn up to develop a new wing of the Foynes Flying Boat Museum dedicated to Maureen O'Hara after the family of the legendary actress, who died October 24, 2015, donated a large collection of memorabilia to the museum. A container load of items belonging to the star has already arrived in Foynes with more to come. According to Margaret O'Shaughnessy, director of the museum, it contains more than fifty dresses, as well as some of her awards, including her 2014 honorary Oscar.

The collection also includes a number of items belonging to and connected with Ms. O'Hara's former husband, Capt. Charles Blair, Pan Am's aviation pioneer who made the first non-stop commercial flight from Europe to New York. In October 1945, he flew his airline's last scheduled flying boat out of Foynes. Among his donated objects is the Harmon International Trophy, which was presented to Blair by President Harry Truman in 1951, in acknowledgement of his contribution to aviation.

Maureen O'Hara Blair. *Courtesy of Foynes Flying Boat Museum.*

Maureen O'Hara was a regular visitor to Foynes and had many friends in the area. In 1989, she officially opened the Flying Boat Museum and remained a patron and loyal supporter for the rest of her life.

"We are blessed, delighted, and thrilled that Maureen O'Hara's family has given us much of her memorabilia," said Margaret, who was a close friend of the actress for more than thirty years. "It is a very exciting development for the museum."

Exhibit at Flying Boat & Maritime Museum. *Courtesy of Foynes Flying Boat Museum.*

sponsored the gala event with hundreds of guests—former Pan Am, B.O.A.C., and American Export airline personnel. Presiding over the ceremonies were Maureen O'Hara and Margaret Heckler, the US Ambassador to Ireland at that time.

The museum's twenty-five dedicated employees welcomed 60,000 visitors in 2016, and in April 2016, we hosted three days of Irish-flavored events for more than 300 former Pan American employees. The Irish Spring Reunion included former cockpit crews, flight attendants, ground personnel, management, Juan Trippe's son Ed and his wife Bobbie, plus the only living passenger from Pacific Clipper's round-the-world odyssey, Merry Barton (see Chapter 7). The mayor of Limerick extended a special welcome to the proud Pan Amers at the opening night cocktail party. Ireland's news media made much ado over each of the reunion events, including a luncheon at the museum, replete with Irish dancing and music.

I'm staggered by the enduring pride and devotion former Pan Am employees hold near and dear—a company that ceased to exist in 1991. I'm still reeling from the success of the 2016 blockbuster Irish Spring Reunion, held in my hometown. I'm now regarded as an honorary Pan Amer, to be embraced by the Pan Am "family" at all future reunions.

The passion of Pan Am reminds me of my own passion, passed down to me by my grandfather's love of aviation and the great flying boats. I hope the Foynes Flying Boat Museum does him proud.

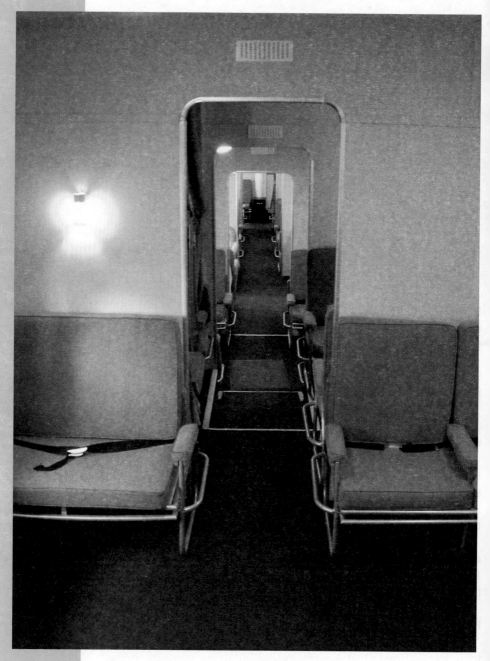

Yankee Clipper full-scale model, passageway.
Courtesy of Foynes Flying Boat Museum.

Epilogue

Teresa Webber

"For once you have tasted flight you will walk the earth with your eyes turned skywards, for there you have been and there you will long to return."

— *Leonardo da Vinci (1452-1519)*

Pan American's stupendous flying boats blazed worldwide routes for less than eleven years, but during that brief time, they played essential roles in the advancement of global economics, lifestyles, politics, the arts, medicine, technology, aviation, and the public's psyche.

Against all odds, when air travel was as farfetched as today's science fiction space fantasies, Juan Trippe and his company turned impossible dreams of air travel into realities.

Gene Roddenberry, creator of *Star Trek*, and Pan Am pilot from 1945 to 1948, could have easily been referring to Pan American in his emblematic tagline, ". . . to boldly go where no one has gone before."

When the Clipper fleet was pressed into service during WWII, their elegant interiors were ripped out, making room for transportation of military personnel and equipment to the European, Pacific, and African fronts. The US Navy and war departments agreed to lease them back to Pan Am for one dollar each. Trippe declined.

By the end of the war, runways had been built at most major destinations all over the world, rendering flying boats obsolete. During that time, the once-glorious Clippers had gone missing, been scrapped, or destroyed by the enemy.

It was the end of a decisive aviation era—and no one knew it better than Pan Am's founder, Juan Trippe.

Listed below is a tribute to those marvelous flying boat machines, their brief histories, and ultimate fates. It is reprinted with permission from *Pan American Clippers—The Golden Age of Flying Boats* by James Trautman (S-38 aircraft not included).

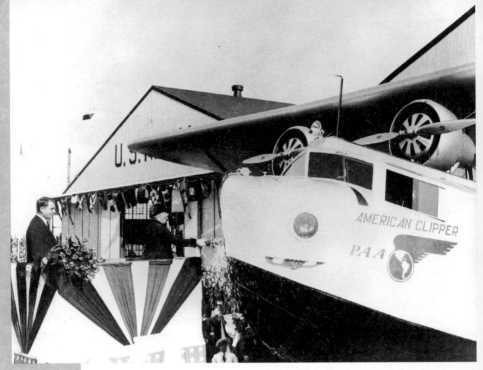

Sikorsky S-40 (3)

NC80V—***American Clipper*** entered service in October 1931. Took the first inaugural flight on November 11, 1931. Served in Latin American and was eventually scrapped.

NC81V—***Caribbean Clipper*** entered service in November 1931. Served in Latin American and was eventually scrapped.

NC752V—***Southern Clipper*** entered service in August 1932. Served in Latin American and was eventually scrapped.

Sikorsky S-42 (10)

NC822M—***Brazilian Clipper*** entered service in May 1934. Served in Latin America. Renamed the ***Colombia Clipper*** and was employed on the Pacific survey flights to chart new routes. Scrapped on July 15, 1946.

NC823M—***West Indies Clipper***, renamed ***Pan American Clipper*** and later ***Hong Kong Clipper***, entered service in December 1934. Employed on Pacific survey flights. Sank at Antilla, Cuba, on August 7, 1944.

NC824M—Never christened or named. Entered service in May 1935. Employed in Latin America. Crashed at Port-au-Spain, Trinidad, on December 20, 1935.

NC15373 (S-42A)—***Jamaica Clipper*** entered service in July 1935. Employed on Latin American flights. Scrapped on July 15, 1946.

NC15374 (S-42A)—*Antilles Clipper* entered service in December 1935. Employed on Latin American flights. Scrapped on July 15, 1946.

NC15375 (S-42A) *Brazilian Clipper* entered service in February 1936. Later renamed the *Colombia Clipper*. Employed on Latin American flights. Scrapped on July 15, 1946. (This is the same flying boat as the NC822M, an S-42. When it went back to Sikorsky to be rebuilt, it emerged from the factory reflagged as an S-42A with upgraded engines, fuel system, autopilot, and wing upgrades. For unknown reasons, Sikorsky registered it with a new tail number.)

NC15376 (S-42A)—*Dominican Clipper* entered service in April 1936. Employed on Latin American flights. Lost in accident in San Juan Harbor, Puerto Rico, on October 3, 1941.

NC16734 (S-42B)—*Pan American Clipper II*, renamed the *Samoan Clipper*, entered service in September 1936. Employed as the survey aircraft for Pan American's chief pilot, Capt. Edwin C. Musick. *Samoan Clipper* was lost with its entire crew on January 11, 1938, near Pago Pago, American Samoa.

NC16735 (S-42B)—*Bermuda Clipper* entered service in September 1936. Served on Atlantic and Pacific routes and the Baltimore to Bermuda route. Renamed the *Alaska Clipper* in 1940, and later the *Hong Kong Clipper II*. Served on the Manila to Hong Kong route. Sunk on December 8, 1941, in Hong Kong Harbor by attacking Japanese aircraft. Became the first American aircraft destroyed in WWII.

NC16736 (S-42B)—*Pan American Clipper III* entered service in 1937. Employed on North and South Atlantic survey flights. Transferred to the Bermuda route in 1940, and renamed the *Bermuda Clipper*. Destroyed at Manaus, Brazil, 1,000 miles up the Amazon River on July 2, 1943.

Martin M-130

NC14716—The *China Clipper* inaugurates the first trans-Pacific airmail service on November 22, 1935 with 111,000 letters on board. It returned to San Francisco on December 6, 1935.

NC14714—The *Hawaii Clipper* inaugurates the first (revenue generating) scheduled transoceanic passenger service between California and the Philippines on October 21, 1936. The round-trip flight was completed on November 4, 1936.

NC-14715—The *Philippine Clipper* inaugurates the first passenger service into Hong Kong on October 14, 1936. A public relations VIP flight, it landed in Hong Kong on October 23 and returned to San Francisco on November 2, 1936.

Boeing 314 (12)

NC18601—*Honolulu Clipper* was the B-314 prototype. Entered service in January 1939. Served Pacific routes. After a forced landing 650 miles from Oahu, it collided with US Navy rescue ship USS *San Pablo* while being towed. Unable to salvage, it was destroyed by US Navy cannon fire on November 11, 1945.

NC18602—*California Clipper*, renamed **Pacific Clipper**, entered service in January 1939. Employed on Pacific routes. Sold to the US Navy in 1942 (Navy Number 48224). Sold to World Airways after WWII. Scrapped in 1950.

NC18603—**Yankee Clipper** entered service in February 1939. Delivered first transatlantic airmail in 1939. Sold to the US Navy in 1942 (Navy Number 48225). Crashed and sank in the River Tagus near Lisbon, Portugal, on February 22, 1943.

NC18604—*Atlantic Clipper* entered service in March 1939. Employed on Atlantic routes. Sold to the US Navy in 1942 (Navy Number 48226). Salvaged for spare parts in 1946.

NC18605—**Dixie Clipper** entered service in April 1939. Employed on Atlantic routes and carried the first transatlantic passengers. Sold to the US Navy in 1942 (Navy Number 48227). Became the first unofficial presidential aircraft when it carried President Roosevelt on his historic flight to Casablanca in January 1943. Sold to World Airways in 1946, and scrapped in 1950.

NC18606—**American Clipper** entered service in June 1939. Employed on Atlantic routes. Sold to the US Army Air Forces in 1942 (Army Air Forces Number 88631). Later sold to the US Navy (Navy Number 99083). Sold to World Airway in 1946. Scrapped in 1950.

Boeing B-314A
Atlantic Clipper.
Courtesy of
PAHF.

NC18607A—Unnamed. Ordered by Pan American Airways but sold to the British government on request from the US government. Entered service in April 1941 (British Purchasing Commission Number 18607). The NC18607A changed to G-AGBZ and the aircraft was named *Bristol*. Sold to World Airways in 1948. Eventually scrapped.

NC18608A—Unnamed. Ordered by Pan American Airways, but sold to the British government on request from the US government. Entered service in April 1941 (British Purchasing Commission Number 18608). The NC18608A changed to G-AGCA, and the aircraft was named *Berwick*. Sold to World Airways in 1948. Eventually scrapped.

NC18609—*Pacific Clipper* entered service in May 1941. Employed on Pacific routes, replacing the *California Clipper*, which was being deployed to Atlantic routes. Sold to the US Army Air Forces (Army Number 42-88632). Later sold to the US Navy in 1946 (Navy Number 99084). Navy sold the aircraft to Universal Airlines. Aircraft damaged in a storm and was salvaged for spare parts.

NC18610A—Unnamed. Ordered by Pan American Airways but sold to the British government on request from the US government. Entered service in April 1941 (British Purchasing Commission Number G-AGCB), and named *Bangor*. Sold to World Airways in 1948. Eventually scrapped.

NC18611A—*Anzac Clipper* entered service in June 1941. Employed on Pacific and Atlantic routes. Sold to the US Army Air Forces (Army Number 88630). Later sold to the US Navy (Navy Number 99082). Sold to American International Airways after WWII. Sold to World Airways in 1948. Sold to unknown parties in 1951, and destroyed in Baltimore, Maryland.

NC18612A—*Cape Town Clipper* entered service in August 1941. Employed on Atlantic routes. Sold to the US Army Air Forces in 1942 (Army Number 42-88622). Later sold to the US Navy (Navy Number 99081). Sold to American International Airways in 1947. Sunk at sea by the US Coast Guard as a hazard after it collided with a boat on October 14, 1947.

Oh! I have slipped the surly bonds of Earth
And danced the skies on laughter-silvered wings;
Sunward I've climbed, and joined the tumbling mirth
Of sun-split clouds,—and done a hundred things
You have not dreamed of—wheeled and soared and swung
   High in the sunlit silence.
Hov'ring there, I've chased the shouting wind along, and flung
My eager craft through footless halls of air . . .
Up, up the long, delirious burning blue
I've topped the wind-swept heights with easy grace
Where never lark, or ever eagle flew . . .

   —*High Flight* by aviator John Gillespie Magee Jr. (1922–1941)

Notes

Foreword
Julia Cooke, childhood memories and reflections about Pan Am.

Introduction
Teresa Webber, Pan Am's military involvement since 1935, email from Pan Am Captain Don Cooper, 2017.

Chapter 1. In the Beginning
Teresa Webber and Jamie Dodson, personal conversations with Edward Trippe about his father, Juan Trippe, 2016.

Chapter 2. Movers & Shakers
Teresa Webber and Jamie Dodson with Jeff Kriendler, personal conversations with Edward Trippe, 2016. Interviews with Frannie Haws, daughter of Sam Pryor, 2016.

Chapter 3. Paving the Way
Jamie Dodson, John Borger taped interview, courtesy Pan Am Historical Foundation.

Chapter 4. The Debut of the *China Clipper*
Robert Gandt (See bibliography for all references).

Chapter 5. Nuts & Bolts
Thomas Kewin, first-person accounts, intimate knowledge of flying boat mechanics and operations during 1930s and 1940s.

Chapter 6. The Long Way Home
Ed Dover, all information provided through author's interviews with *Pacific Clipper* Captain Robert Ford in 1992 and 1993, and with Radio Operator Eugene Leach.

Chapter 7. Rescue from Noumea
Merry Barton, childhood memories of her family's evacuation from Noumea on *Pacific Clipper* in 1941.

Chapter 8. Flying Boat Memoirs
Robert Hicks, excerpts from his personal logs.

Chapter 9. Pan Am at War
Reprinted with permission from PanAm.org/PAHF and Robert Gandt.

Chapter 10. The Art Deco Era of Pan Am Terminals
James Trautman, "Landmarks Preservation Committee," November 25, 1980, referencing documents and reports on New York Marine Air Terminal and background on architect William Delano.

Chapter 11: The Dreamboats: Flying in Style
Clare Luce quote: www.allgreatquotes.com.

Rebecca Sprecher and Dian Groh, draft of article about Betsy Schafer's flight aboard the *Atlantic Clipper*, July 5, 1939. "William A. Winston" file. Pan Am archives, Richter Library, University of Miami.

Chapter 12: Flying Back in Time
Marcus Aurelius Antonius quote: *Bartlett's Familiar Quotations*, from his *Meditations*, IV, 43. Little Brown and Co., 2002.

Rebecca Sprecher with Dian Groh, *Guam Eagle, October 14, 1935*. Cover story re arrival of Pan Am Sikorsky S-42. Pan Am archives, Richter Library, University of Miami.

Article about repairing damaged *Pacific Clipper*. Unspecified Long Beach, California, newspaper, Walter Case, Dec. 15, 1942. Pan Am archives, Richter Library, University of Miami.

Horace Brock, *Flying the Oceans: A Pilot's Story of Pan Am* (Stinehour Press, Lunenburg, VT, Third edition), 134.

"William A. Winston" file, *Pacific Clipper* crew layover in Lagos, Nigeria, while on secret mission to transport King George II of Greece to Baltimore. Pan Am archives, Richter Library, University of Miami.

"Boeing 314 History, Part II: Boeing Clippers' War Time Activity." Internal document. 15. Pan Am archives, Richter Library, University of Miami.

Atlantic Division: Sample list of "Prominent Military and Diplomatic Passengers Essential to War Effort, Outgoing from USA." 1–5. Pan Am archives, Richter Library, University Miami.

Chapter 13. Off the Beaten Track: A Museum Like No Other
Margaret O'Shaughnessy, first-person account and history of the Foynes Flying Boat Museum.

"Air and Space." Edwin Musick. www.airandspace.ai.edu, 2015.

Airliners. www.airliners.net, 2015.

Biography. "Anne Morrow Lindbergh." 2www.biography.com, 2015.

Biography. "Igor Sikorsky." www.biography.com, 2015.

Birger, Larry. "Pan Am Pioneers Recall Early Days" (re steward Joey Carrero). *Miami News Reporter,* October 1977.

Brock, Horace. *Flying the Oceans: A Pilot's Story of Pan Am, 1935–1955.* Rev. ed. Lanham, MD: Jason Aronson, May 1983.

Charles Lindbergh. "Charles Lindbergh Biography." "Juan Trippe (1899–1981). Biography." Branson, Richard. www.charleslindbergh. com, 2015.

China National Aviation Corporation. "André A. Priester." www.cnac. org, 2015.

Clipper Flying Boats. www.clipperflyingboats.com, 2015.

Cohen, Stan. *Wings to the Orient: A Pictorial History.* Missoula, MT: Pictorial History Publishing Company, 1996.

Daley, Robert. *An American Saga: Juan Trippe and His Pan Am Empire.* New York: Random House, 1980.

Dover, Ed. *The Long Way Home.* Rev. ed. Albuquerque, NM: Ed Dover, 2008.

Early Aviators. "Edwin C. Musick." www.earlyaviators.com, accessed 2015.

earharttruth (blog). December 23, 2014. "Amelia Earhart: The Truth at Last." "Fred Noonan: Amelia Earhart's Forgotten Navigator," https:// earharttruth.wordpress.com.

Encyclopedia Britannica (online). "Igor Sikorsky." www.britannica.com, 2015.

Eugene McDermott Library, University of Texas at Dallas. Edwin C. Musick Collection. www.utdallas.edu, 2014.

Everything Pan Am. Kelly Cusak, webmaster. www.everythingpanam. com. 2014–16.

Flying Clippers. Michael McKinney, webmaster. www.flyingclippers. com. 2014–16.

Foynes Flying Boat and Maritime Museum Archives. www. flyingboatmuseum.com. 2014–16.

Follett, Ken. *Night over Water*. New York: Signet Books, 1992.

Fowler, Glenn. "John C. Leslie, 76, Pan Am Executive." *New York Times*, Jan. 23, 1982. www.nytimes.com.

Gandt, Robert. *China Clipper: The Age of the Great Flying Boats*. New York: Naval Institute Press, 1991.

Gandt, Robert. *Skygods: The Fall of Pan Am*. New York: William Morrow, 1995.

Greenough, "Shorty." Article on Sampan Annie. *New Horizons*, Pan Am monthly magazine, September, 1941.

Grooch, William Stephen. *From Crate to Clipper*. New York: Longmans, Green & Co., 1936.

Grooch, William Stephen. *Skyway To Asia*. New York: Longmans, Green & Co., 1936.

History. "Amelia Earhart's Navigator: The Life and Loss of Fred Noonan." www.history.com, 2015.

History. "The Great Depression—Facts & Summary." www.history.com, 2015.

Inc. "The Great Leaders Series: Juan Trippe, Founder of Pan American Airways." 2015. www.inc.com.

Kauffman, Sanford B. *Pan Am Pioneer: A Manager's Memoir*. Lubbock: Texas Tech University Press, 1995, 163–164.

Krupnick, Jon E. *Pacific Pioneers, the Rest of the Story: A Pictorial History of Pan Am's First Fights, 1935–1945*. Missoula, MT: Pictorial History Publishing, 2000.

Larson, George C. *Airspace Smithsonian Magazine* (online). Re Glenn L. Martin, "Moments And Milestones: Birth of the Clippers." www.airspace.com, 2011.

Leslie, Peter. *Aviation's Quiet Pioneer: Pan American Flying Boats*. CreateSpace, March, 2012.

Musick Point Radio Group and Musick Memorial Radio Station. 2015. www.musickpointradio.org.

National Aviation Hall Of Fame. Igor Sikorsky. 2015. www. nationalaviation.org.

Pan Am Historical Foundation. Doug Miller, webmaster. "John Leslie: PAA Pioneer." "Hugo Leuteritz." "What We Owe to Musick". "Andre Priester." "Igor Sikorsky." "The Very First Clippers." "Juan Trippe." 2014–16. www.panam.org.

PBS. "The American Experience: Anne Morrow Lindbergh." 2015. www.
pbs.org.

PBS. "They Made America: Juan Trippe." 2014. www.pbs.org.

Priester, André. "Pilot Conduct" found in "Operations Manual: Pan
American Airways System." Pan Am archives, Richter Library,
University of Miami.

Seattle, Pacific Northwest Aviation Historical Foundation. "Dreamboat:
Wellwood Beall and the Boeing Clipper," 1979.

SFO Museum. Julie Takata, curator. www.flysfo.com, 2015.

Sikorsky Archives. 2014. www.sikorskyarchives.com.

Smith, J. Y. "Juan Trippe, Pan Am Founder Dies." *Washington Post*, April
1981.

Smithsonian National Air and Space Museum: John A. Hambleton.
https://airandspace.si.edu, 2015.

Stettinius, Betty. *Pan Am's First Lady: The Diary of Betty Stettinius
Trippe*. McLean, VA: Paladwr, 1996.

TIGHAR. International Group for Historic Aircraft Recovery. "The
Earhart Project: Fred Noonan," Hamilton, Jerry. https://tighar.org,
2015.

Trautman, James. *Pan American Clippers: The Golden Age of Flying
Boats*. Boston: Boston Mills Press, 2011.

University of Miami Special Collections website. "Cleared to Land: The
Records of the Pan American World Airways, Inc." 2014. www.
scholar.library.miami.edu.

Ward, Colm. "Maureen O'Hara Memorabilia Donation to Flying Boat
Museum." *Limerick Leader*, July 24, 2016.

Weintz, Steve. War Is Boring (blog). "How America's Airline Went to
War." 2014. www.wrisboring.com.

Wikipedia: "Art Deco Elements." Last modified November 24, 2016.
https:/en.wikipedia.org.

Wikipedia: "Boeing 314 Clipper." Last modified November 19, 2016.
https://en.wikipedia.org.

Wikipedia: "Consolidated Commodore." Last modified February 21,
2016. https://en.wikipedia.org.

Wikipedia: "Sikorsky Aircraft." Last modified November 13, 2016.
https://en.wikipedia.org.

Wikipedia: "Tex Johnston." Last modified October 11, 2016. https://en.
wikipedia.org.

"Who Made America?" 2014. www.pbs.org.

Index